UPSCALE DOWNSIZING

UPSCALE DOWNSIZING

CREATING A
STYLISH, ELEGANT,
SMALLER HOME

BY LESLIE LINSLEY

STERLING
New York

STERLING
New York

An Imprint of Sterling Publishing Co., Inc.
1166 Avenue of the Americas
New York, NY 10036

ISBN 978-1-4549-2197-4

Distributed in Canada by Sterling Publishing Co., Inc.
C/o Canadian Manda Group, 664 Annette Street
Toronto, Ontario, Canada M6S 2C8
Distributed in the United Kingdom by GMC Distribution Services
Castle Place, 166 High Street, Lewes, East Sussex, England BN7 1XU
Distributed in Australia by NewSouth Books
45 Beach Street, Coogee, NSW 2034, Australia

For information about custom editions, special sales, and premium and corporate purchases, please contact Sterling Special Sales at 800-805-5489 or specialsales@sterlingpublishing.com.

Manufactured in Canada

2 4 6 8 10 9 7 5 3 1

sterlingpublishing.com

Design by Chris Thompson and Sharon Jacobs
Photo credits on page 196.

A home is an expression of our personalities, and

as we change our lifestyles, we are able to change the

way our home responds to and fosters that lifestyle.

A home is an integral part of who we are.

Your home tells your story.

INTRODUCTION

I have been writing about stylish homes and the people who own them for a long time, both for magazine articles and as the subject of my books. I live on Nantucket Island, Massachusetts, where people tend to furnish their homes with an awareness of good design. Along with writing about different architectural styles and houses of every size, I have most enjoyed interviewing the homeowners who have decorated small homes with imagination and describing how they found clever, practical, and stylish ways to solve everyday living problems. I also spend a great deal of time in Key West, Florida, and write about the small cottages on that island. Again, I have been fortunate to find creative people who have allowed me to come into their homes to photograph and write about them. It has given me an appreciation for living small with upscale taste.

When my book *Nantucket Cottages & Gardens* was published, I was invited to give many talks about the featured houses and the lifestyles of the homeowners. During this time, I was often approached by people in the audience who asked questions about how to downsize without compromising their good tastes. Many lived in large homes filled with treasures, both acquired and inherited, and could not imagine how to either get rid of things they cherished, or figure out how to use everything in a smaller home. This gave me the idea for a book showing rooms designed for different lifestyle situations, along with tips and suggestions for solving basic problems. I wanted to show interesting homes minimally, as well as abundantly, furnished. It presented an interesting challenge to find people, in all different situations and parts of the country, who had not only downsized but who had also made their new, smaller homes exquisitely interesting without compromise. Most of them said that it was a liberating experience and an opportunity to redefine and express themselves anew. I have many friends who are internationally known interior designers. I asked them for input on small projects they had designed, and they graciously provided material that demonstrates how they helped some of their clients downsize in style.

ELEGANT STYLE OFTEN COMES IN A DECIDEDLY LOW-KEY GUISE— UNDERSTATED & UNEXPECTEDLY COMFORTABLE.

DOWNSIZING ISN'T RELATED TO AGE

There are many reasons for downsizing living space, but, as you will see, this process doesn't have to mean downgrading. Downsizing can be extremely freeing at any stage of life, particularly at the beginning of a new chapter. Sometimes downsizing occurs due to circumstances that force a move, and sometimes it's a choice. One thing I've learned is that downsizing is not age-related. For example, two young women I know who had been college roommates shared their first

apartment, a one-bedroom, after graduation. A year later, one moved to another part of the country. Unable to find someone to take her place in the apartment and unable to pay the full rent alone, the remaining friend was forced to downsize to a studio apartment.

Perhaps a career has escalated to the point where there isn't the time, desire, or interest in taking care of a home and property. Or perhaps it's a time in one's life when travel is an option. Maybe the children have left home and the need for space isn't what it once was. Or perhaps moving to a more expensive area calls for space compromises.

Many people say, "Less space means more leisure time." Some young couples are embracing the idea of the "tiny house concept"—a small house on wheels for flexible living. "We decided to spend more time traveling and doing things other than taking care of a house, and we didn't want a big mortgage," said a newlywed couple with whom I spoke.

Downsizing, however, doesn't have to mean living in a humble abode, especially if the person, couple, or family has spent a lifetime accumulating lovely things or has a sense of style. That college graduate took the shabby-chic approach and created a delightfully feminine room. "My friends always hang out here," she says, "because my apartment feels like the homes we all grew up in."

"Once our children were grown and out of the nest," said one woman with three adult offspring, "we looked around and asked ourselves what we were doing with such a big home." Many empty-nesters, retirees, and people whose circumstances have changed are ready for a different lifestyle. Taking care of a house may not be part of the plan. They often want to be more involved with their communities.

A widower with a three-bedroom apartment in the suburbs decided to downsize to a one-bedroom apartment in the city. He wanted a place that would represent his new status as a single man with sophisticated taste. He had been hesitant to move because he had so many beautiful antiques that couldn't possibly fit into a smaller home. The urge to change his life ultimately became more compelling than keeping all his things. It was time to divest and become selective.

My grandmother, who was an artist, frequently rearranged the rooms in her small home. She enjoyed making it look new and different, and changing the artwork was part of this activity. On her ninetieth birthday, she announced that she had done all the rearranging she could do and still find pleasure in her home. She sold the house and moved to a three-room apartment where she could start over again. "I always want to be the oldest thing in my house," she often proclaimed, and perfecting her little nest was something that gave her joy to the end of her life at 101.

An Oregon couple had a yearning for adventure, the kind they'd had before they were married and owned a large home. Feeling tied down by their

mortgage, they decided to downsize in order to free up time and money for travel. They felt that the "bigger is better" mentality didn't work anymore. Their plan included top-of-the-line materials (hardwood floors), fixtures (aged, bronze, barn-style sconces), and finishes (hand-hewn pine beams), creating an affordable house that wouldn't skimp on style or quality. They built their home to their exact design and said, "Having less has given us so much more."

Making a nest as comfortable and as visually pleasing as possible is an ongoing process that has nothing to do with the size of one's home. Many people who live in a 1,000-square-foot (92.9-square-meter) home agree. Some homeowners find that downsizing offers a new lease on life, especially if they've owned a larger home for many years. They sell or give away all their furnishings and start from scratch, infusing their space with a sophistication that was no longer possible in their old home.

THE ART OF DOWNSIZING WELL

Elegance is cultivated and not something that is purchased overnight, no matter what a well-meaning decorator tells you. But a home or room can exude touches of elegance with the right fabric, a small detail, like silk tassels on pillows, or a tapestry tablecloth. Downsizing elegantly is an art you can learn. Furthermore, furnishing a small home with style is easy to do on a budget. You need less, so you can buy quality. Today, there are more sources than ever for finding just the right furnishings, antiques and good reproductions, artwork, accessories, and stylish hardware and fixtures to create an upscale, exciting, and interesting home. It's easy to incorporate what you already own and love with what is newly on the market.

I bought an old Oriental rug for my living room. While it gives the room more character than it deserves, it makes my white loveseats and chairs look outstanding.

Good planning is essential when furnishing small spaces. Every square inch counts, and most people can't afford to make impulsive buys on things that don't solve problems or add to the beauty and comfort of their homes. However, if letting a home evolve is more your style than instant decorating, that can work, too. And, if you're on a strict budget, you can now find things that are shockingly inexpensive. You don't have to be afraid to make a mistake, because almost everything is returnable.

Internationally known interior designer Christina Roughan has offices in Weston, Connecticut, and New York City. Known for her timeless and tailored spaces, Christina believes that interiors are to be lived in and should reflect the people who reside in them. Her advice: "Every interior should be functional while remaining aesthetically purposeful and elegant."

OPPOSITE:

Modern fixtures, sink, cabinets, and countertops easily make an ordinary bathroom upscale. This was part of an urban apartment renovation designed by Roughan Interior Design.

BELOW:

The wall of a one-bedroom loft apartment was removed in this apartment to create an open kitchen, eating area, and living room. A piece of furniture helps distinguish the living room from the eating area. The front side, facing the living-room area, is used for storage, and a bench sits against the back, facing the dining area and kitchen. The neutral color palette unifies the space, making it seem larger, while the punctuation of one or two bright accents makes it lively. A sectional sofa is a good solution for creating adequate seating in the living room as well.

THE UPSIDE TO DOWNSIZING

Aside from less maintenance, lower utility bills, and more leisure time, there are many advantages to downsizing. Chances are high that, when moving into a smaller space, you have a little more money to spend on upgrades. And if you've already lived elsewhere, you've been able to hone your taste. You may not know exactly what you *want*, but most of us know what we *don't* want.

Upgrade Appliances

Many kitchens and bathrooms in older homes need upgrading. This can be an opportunity to use the sleekest, most modern materials without compromise. One homeowner, an avid cook, says, "The real challenge in laying out a small kitchen is figuring out how to accommodate favorite luxuries,

OPPOSITE:

A woman who lives by herself in a one-room apartment (and who rarely entertains) delineated an eating corner with carefully chosen items: a narrow cabinet, plates on the wall, a small table and chairs, and a low lamp for soft lighting (no overhead lights). All-white chinaware rather than busy patterns are used for a small area.

ABOVE:

Dark-stained beams were added to the ceiling of this duplex home to visually define the kitchen and dining areas. The counter stools, dining table, and chairs, as well as countertops, contrast nicely with the light walls and wood floors to keep the space from looking too sterile.

like a Wolf® oven and a Sub-Zero® refrigerator, extra-deep pot drawers, and an ample pantry." However, more money can be spent on things like better fixtures and appliances to make small look upscale. There are fewer compromises to be made when buying things for the way you really want to live.

Don't overlook a tiny area as the perfect spot for a little table and a sweet bouquet. It's totally unexpected!

A huge collection of country crocks and pitchers was whittled down to fit neatly into a dry sink in a country kitchen. Together, they make a nice utilitarian display.

Knowing Where Everything Is

A small home doesn't swallow things. You know where they are. When you live small, you should love everything you put in a room. One homeowner said, "I like all the rooms lit at night so the entire house becomes an integral part of life. With a large house, you tend to live in just parts of it, never lighting all the rooms at once. You can afford to have nice furnishings and accessories. When you live small, it gives you a chance to really figure out what you want in each room. What is essential? It's also easy to arrange pretty things and perfect your environment when your home is small."

Your downsized home speaks for itself. Anything that is out of place will immediately and obviously look "wrong." Once you're set up, it's easy to keep things tidy. It's easier if you can be very clear about what you can live without and what is essential to your well-being before you move in. It's so much harder to divest after the fact. You might want to identify why something is occupying the space when space is at a premium.

Details Mean a Lot

A smaller home can be enhanced by special details and designed to perfectly accommodate the lifestyle of its occupants. Neither size nor volume has anything to do with style and comfort. The small-home concept works when superfluous square footage is traded for less tangible but more meaningful aspects of design. These may include window seats, built-ins, decorative woodwork, efficient top-of-the-line appliances, and accessories that add quality to the use and look of the rooms.

Downsizing often requires creative thinking for choosing and arranging furniture, finding adequate storage space, displaying collections, hanging artwork, entertaining, outfitting a small kitchen, and, in general, making decisions about what to keep and what to toss depending on how you will use it. Decluttering seems to be the hardest for most of us. Laying out rooms in a downsized home can be harder than furnishing larger rooms, but the results are often more satisfying for the effort.

As a journalist, I'm used to editing words. Editing makes the idea or subject of an article stronger. The same is true with objects. I've always loved the following quote from my favorite author E. B. White. He wrote, in a letter to a friend, "Pardon this lengthy letter. I haven't the time to be brief." Brevity can be an asset for all who want to downsize.

The idea of downsizing with an upscale attitude is very exciting and presents a wonderful opportunity to define, or perhaps redefine, yourself. You can create a perfect nest for your current, as well as future, lifestyle.

YOUR
BIGGEST SAVINGS?
TIME . . .

FROM LESS MAINTENANCE TO FEWER DECISIONS! THOSE WHO DOWNSIZE SAY THEY FEEL MORE CONNECTED TO THEIR COMMUNITIES BECAUSE THEY HAVE MORE TIME AND MONEY TO GET OUT AND DO THINGS. THEY OFTEN VOLUNTEER.

MY SMALL-HOME EXPERIENCES

Over the years, I have lived in more than thirty-five different houses, cottages, and apartments, both for short-term stays—as little as ten days in a country home in the south of France and three weeks in an oversize apartment in Florence, Italy—to those lasting two or three years. I rented vacation homes in Key West, Florida, for as short as two weeks or as long as three months; I lived in a 1,200-square-foot (111-square-meter) apartment in New York City that I rented and then owned for fifteen years; I subleased a one-room studio in Beacon Hill, Boston, a few years ago when I owned a store in the neighborhood. Some of those homes were one- to three-room apartments, and some houses had three bedrooms. My husband and I rented a huge house for nine months while building our current home. But most of the places I've lived in were no larger than the home I now own—approximately 2,200 square feet (204 square meters), of which I use about half now that my children are grown. We use different rooms at different times, depending on the work we're currently doing. I say "we" as my husband, a graphic designer and photographer, and I have always worked together. As you'll discover throughout the book, we're do-it-yourselfers, so our life is filled with projects that come with a prerequisite: "Some assembly required."

Throughout the experience of living in each space, for however short or long a period, I have made it my own as fast as possible. I do this quickly so that I can get back to the flow of my suspended life and enjoy the space I've created. I've always made a valiant attempt to respond to my aesthetic sense of well-being and my level of comfort. I've never liked to "make do." The amount of time that I will be in a space often determines how much time, effort, and money I expend, but as a general rule I spend as little as possible!

When I stay in temporary spaces, I buy lots of inexpensive candles in votive holders to create soft lighting and disguise anything unappealing, like a worn sofa or scuffed table. The lighting makes a huge difference, and I'm quite sensitive to that aspect of a place. Brightly lit rooms are often uninviting. I buy a high-wattage light bulb for a lamp I will use for working at my computer and pink or low-wattage bulbs for ambience. When there are no dimmers on living-room lamps, I buy a plug-in cord made for this purpose.

My experience has taught me that, in small spaces, there's usually too much furniture. I rearrange as best I can, always taking pictures of the room beforehand so I can put everything back

OPPOSITE:

A loft bedroom was created above half of the living room and is reached by an open ironwork stairway. Two curved sofas and a round coffee table provide ample space for the single owner, who rotates the artwork from time to time. "I have more objects than space," he says. "It's easy to change them often when the room becomes boring."

the way it was. I am big on leaving no footprint. The same is true when I style a room for a photographic shoot. When I choose a home to feature, it's because I have respect for the homeowner's or designer's taste, so I try to impose as little of my aesthetic as possible, except when I know that slight adjustments or the arrangement of flowers will result in a better photograph.

When I rent a home, I remove the homeowner's personal effects, like framed family photographs, and always replace them with fresh flowers from the supermarket (a big bang for the buck!). I streamline as much as possible.

I've found that inexpensive plastic storage boxes do a great job of controlling clutter that isn't mine and are good for containing all my work material in one place, which is sometimes under the dining table where I've set up "shop." In other words, whether you're living in a temporary furnished sublet or downsizing for the short term, the first thing to do is clean up any extraneous things, camouflage what isn't instantly working for you, and then, if you plan an extended stay, you can develop a long-term plan. But first, before making this space your own, you have to create a somewhat impersonal canvas.

I chose to write this bit of advice before delving into the complex business of downsizing for real—that is, settling into your own home and doing it in style—because there's nowhere to go from here but up. Now the fun begins. This is a journey that will change your life. You're moving down in size and up in style because it is the right direction, right now, for you. Embrace this time. It's like a first kiss, a first "I love you." There is only one "first."

LEFT:

The chandelier, crown molding, high ceilings, and tall windows make the room seem spacious.

FROM A WOMAN WHO LIVES ALONE

"A SMALLER HOME MAKES ME FEEL SAFE. IT'S COZY, WELCOMING, AND REASSURING TO BE ABLE TO SEE FROM ONE ROOM TO THE NEXT."

FROM A MAGAZINE EDITOR

"I LOVE BOOKS AND MAGAZINES AS ACCESSORIES, EVEN THOUGH A TABLET TAKES UP LESS ROOM. I PILE BOOKS HERE AND THERE. THEY MAKE ROOMS PERSONAL. THERE ARE ALWAYS BOOKS ON MY COFFEE TABLE. IT'S NOT CLUTTER. IT'S PART OF MY LIFESTYLE AND THEREFORE MY 'DECORATING' STYLE."

FROM A SHELTER-MAGAZINE JUNKIE

"I GET COMFORT FROM PERUSING BEAUTIFULLY PHOTOGRAPHED ROOMS AND THEN PICKING OUT DETAILS TO RE-CREATE IN MY OWN HOME. A WORD OF CAUTION: CHOOSE YOUR ACCESSORIES CAREFULLY. THAT'S EXACTLY WHAT THEY ARE: ACCESSORIES, NOT NECESSITIES, AND SHOULD BE CHOSEN LAST, AS THE ICING ON THE CAKE. ASK YOURSELF, 'HOW DOES EACH ITEM MAKE ME FEEL?' INDIFFERENT? PUT IT ASIDE."

FROM A DO-IT-YOURSELFER

"WHEN I WANT A CHANGE IN MY SMALLER HOME, IT'S EASY TO EITHER PAINT A PIECE OF FURNITURE, OR MOVE THINGS AROUND."

FROM A MOTHER OF GROWN CHILDREN

"I NO LONGER PICK UP AFTER OTHERS, AND MY UTILITY BILLS ARE MUCH SMALLER."

FROM A WIDOW

"I HAVE FEWER THINGS TO PUT AWAY."

FROM A NEWLYWED COUPLE

"WE HAVE MORE TIME FOR FUN ACTIVITIES TOGETHER."

PART I

EDIT! EDIT! EDIT!

When deciding to downsize, the first question that may come to mind is, *How will I fit my things into a smaller space? Where will the sectional sofa or king-size bed go?* While these may seem like looming problems, these chapters offer tips to help you assess what you can or can't live without and suggest new, creative ways to use what you have. You'll find advice for weeding out things you don't need or love. You'll learn how to adapt your lifestyle without compromising your style and taste. For example, if you had a formal dining room but now have only a breakfast nook, you might choose to casually entertain—but still use your nicest silver and table linens. Be inspired and learn how you can have fun while changing your lifestyle.

1

LOVE IT OR LOSE IT

Divesting yourself of what you don't need or what won't fit in your downsized home is difficult. We always want to keep more rather than less. This very important elimination process, no matter how coldheartedly one approaches it, always gets sticky. There comes a point during this "editing" when you get stuck. For the first few minutes, you are ruthless, throwing away a rusty vegetable peeler and a melon baller ("When have I ever used that?"), but then you get down to the nitty-gritty, the really big stuff, like chairs and a sofa or chest of drawers. However you approach this task, eventually it will need to get done, or you'll be left squeezing too much into too little space. I had a friend who was moving from a large house to a two-bedroom apartment in another state. When the movers showed up at his door and he looked at the size of the truck, he suddenly realized, after months of divesting, that what he had left would never fit into his new apartment.

If you think more is better, you'll realize what a fool you've been when you actually move into your new downsized home, paying to move stuff that doesn't fit. It's harder to get rid of things after you move than before.

So let's get down to it. When I express an idea in writing, I edit sentences so that I'm left with only those words that will get my point across in the most effective way. Think of editing objects using the same process.

OPPOSITE:
A new homeowner had a wall-to-wall unit built at one end of his living room to house books and an assortment of selected items on the top shelves. With closed cabinets below the shelves, he has ample storage space to keep the room sleek and modern, just as he wanted.

When you get rid of extraneous words, you strengthen the thought. The same is true with material possessions. The less you have, the more impact the remaining items will make. Every move is emotional. That's a fact. If you can't bear to get rid of the blown-glass heart you received on your first anniversary, don't. But that "perfectly good" sofa that you've enjoyed for many years but is now all wrong for your new home is not worth pondering over. You'll have your answers if you ask yourself two questions: "Is it worth spending money to restore it?" and "Will it fit comfortably into my new space?"

IT IS NOT THAT HARD: LETTING GO

The usual advice for people who are downsizing is: "Force yourself to get rid of things." Most people who live in small homes say: "You simply can't waste space on anything that isn't useful, comfortable, or visually pleasing." If you want a comfortable house, it's sometimes important to let go of things so you don't feel claustrophobic and choked by your possessions. However, editing isn't just about discarding things. It is really a matter of getting rid of what isn't important to your lifestyle and decorating scheme. What you keep *must* contribute to your sense of well-being. Try this exercise. Look at a table holding a bunch of things. You're allowed to keep only two of them. Which two can you not live without?

When I moved from one state to another, I put lots of furniture and collections in storage. Three years later, I was still paying to store those things and couldn't even remember what they were. Ultimately, I ended up throwing everything away. A good lesson was learned. What you don't take with you might not be worth holding on to.

However, streamlining isn't always the ultimate goal. As you've seen from some of the homeowners I've interviewed, not everyone wants to live minimally. Some people derive pleasure by surrounding themselves with memorabilia. They find comfort in living with the things they've amassed over the years. And with good reason. When a former museum curator and art collector retired, he filled every square inch, including the ceilings of his tiny cottage, with paintings. No longer able to travel, his world began to shrink. He needed to be surrounded with beauty and memories. "It's my personal museum," he said. "My world has gotten smaller. I spend my time at home, and I am transported when I sit and remember." If this resonates with you, then you have to become really good at arranging your belongings to make them look artful. For some people, when their environment gets smaller, this rearrangement of their cherished possessions is like creating a larger world within the space. Working on the interior design can become a meaningful and very satisfying occupation. But for the majority of people moving to a smaller space, editing, decluttering, and substituting becomes a necessity in order to live comfortably.

Editing is just that. Pick and choose what makes a statement, what adds comfort to your life, what is pleasing to look at, what says something about you, and what fits in with your lifestyle. Minimal, cozy, traditional, country-style, eclectic—you decide. But don't keep things just because you have them. It can be extremely liberating to start anew with a reinvented image that is expressed through your environment and, ultimately, to begin a different lifestyle that is well suited for your new situation.

TIP: You can never have too much storage space, so one large dresser is a good item to keep.

CHOOSING BETWEEN THIS OR THAT

Some downsizers can't wait to start over. They want everything to be new, and a smaller space offers them the opportunity to do so without spending a fortune. Out with the chipped cups, mismatched kitchen chairs, stained linens, and makeshift everything and anything. The antique furniture is sold, except for one or two cherished pieces. For these individuals, it really is liberating to re-create or reinvent your lifestyle.

Then there are others who want to downsize for a maintenance-free lifestyle but can't quite let go of the old to embrace the new. So how do you do that? You've lived in the larger space long enough to know what you like and what you are not in love with anymore. You know which sentimental items you simply can't part with. Be honest with yourself.

Internationally known, award-winning interior designer Kathleen Hay says, "There are so many new and elegant materials on the market that once you begin to expose yourself to what's out there, it's so much fun to fantasize about the possibilities. New furnishings and materials are exciting and often function better than the old versions. Once you start imagining a home with these items in it, you can often let go of what you have. The things you held near and dear become less important. You realize you have to move on if you want to achieve your goal."

The following are some basic ideas for furnishing and decorating your new space. They're worth thinking about as you assess what you have, the place you are leaving, and where you will arrive.

➡ If your new space needs painting, do so before you move a single thing.

➡ Interior designers who once favored beige and various shades of white are suddenly opting for gray. One of my favorite shades is "Down Pipe" from Farrow & Ball, an upscale British paint and wallpaper company. When used on all four walls, this gray provides a rich contemporary atmosphere

ABOVE: **Accents of black enliven the scheme.**

to a room and creates a mysteriously moody interior. In an about-face, Farrow & Ball suggests using it on a front door to make it feel a little warmer than if it were just painted black. The color is soft and approachable, the way a front door should be, and is perfect with white trim. These paints are available wherever fine paints are sold worldwide. If you want a more affordable choice, use the Farrow & Ball paint chips to find similar colors from a less expensive paint brand.

➡ The largest pieces of furniture, like the sofa and chairs, should be light in color so they don't overpower the room.

➡ You've taken a lifetime to amass a collection you love. Choose the very best and pack away the others for rotating in the future. Plan out how you will display the items you keep. Group the best of the collection together according to color, size, texture, shape, and subject matter, rather than scattering it about. This will dramatize a collection and make a statement of importance even when mixing old and new. Don't try to jam as much together as possible (unless that makes you happy). It might be worth trying to go for a pleasing arrangement. Once you've

TEN TIPS FOR GETTING STARTED

BEFORE MOVING INTO A SMALLER SPACE THAN THE ONE YOU CURRENTLY INHABIT, YOU'LL WANT TO GET RID OF THE THINGS THAT YOU WON'T NEED OR WANT. THESE DECISIONS CAN BE DIFFICULT TO MAKE. STARTING SMALL BY GETTING RID OF THINGS THAT ARE WORN OUT OR HAVE OUTLIVED THEIR USEFULNESS IS EASIER THAN MAKING DECISIONS THAT TAKE MORE TIME AND CONSIDERATION. HERE ARE A FEW SUGGESTIONS TO HELP YOU WITH YOUR EDITING PROCESS.

1 Where you begin the business of editing is up to you. There really isn't a right or wrong way, but time and distance for the move may be factors to consider before you begin. If possible, create a plan for each area of your home.

2 Tackle one room at a time. If you don't know where to go first, try beginning with the kitchen. Why?

Because it's usually the easiest to edit. Anyone can get rid of things like stained dishtowels and duplicate mixing tools.

3 Begin with one drawer at a time so you won't have your things spread over the kitchen counter all at once and suddenly become overwhelmed by the process. Stop when you can't go on.

4 Next, tackle the closets. Begin with seasonal clothes that no longer fit or those items that you haven't worn in two years. The linen closet should be easy. New sheets and towels are fun to buy for a new home. If you haven't refurbished your linen closet in years, don't even think about keeping the linens unless the sheets still look fabulous.

RIGHT:

A pantry was a luxury in this large family home and provided plenty of room for a massive collection of china. Collected over a lifetime, the china is used and cherished for its reminders of family gatherings over past years. Sometimes it's necessary to find a way to house it all.

6

5 For larger rooms like the bedroom, living room, dining room, or den, focus on one area and eliminate all you can. When you're finished with one area, move on to another section until you've edited the entire room. You can return to each individual area later for a second pass, and maybe even a third.

6 Accessories like lamps, lampshades, vases, or knickknacks are decidedly difficult to throw away. This can be done by having a yard sale, donating to worthy charitable organizations, or going to the dump. Don't get bogged down with the question: "What if I need this in my new home?" You've already answered that.

7 Furniture is the last to be eliminated. Since it can be costly to replace, begin by measuring every room in the new home and be practical about what you can and cannot fit into it. In the end, that old saying "less is more" will serve you well.

8 Window treatments rarely transition well from one home to another, for the following reasons: The window dimensions will probably be different, the views are different, and undoubtedly the interior design style won't be the same. Unless you are very attached to the curtains you lovingly stitched for your bedroom, let them go.

9 Finally, you have to decide what goes on the walls. Most wall decor can be worked into a new scheme, and what doesn't fit or look good can be eliminated later. You can leave these decisions until after your furniture is in place. Floor coverings may not present much of a problem, either. They fit in size, pattern, and color, or they don't.

10 If you have a garage, attic, or basement, you'll need fortitude to deal with it. There are photo albums, trophies, and all the prom dresses that will never again be worn. If you need help, call 1-800-GOT-JUNK? for an estimate. This company removes anything and everything you don't want.

LEFT:
Garages and attics can cause a headache, but you probably don't need to take that sled with you from your Vermont home to your new home in Florida.

got a display, take one piece away and do it again. You can always change objects out with the seasons or when you need a new look.

⮕ Don't hesitate to buy a reproduction of an antique item if it is well designed. When mixed with a good antique, the reproduction will be elevated to a higher status and look more authentic. But while one good antique gives a room character, a whole room filled with brown antique furniture (think mahogany and maple) can look old and heavy.

⮕ When building from scratch, plan the window placements for maximum natural light. You can always create privacy with shutters, shades, blinds, draperies, or curtains.

⮕ However, if you prefer a cocoon-like space, think cozy—not cramped. Try to choose items based on

how they add warmth to the room. Consider earth tones and perhaps a collection of handmade crafts, such as pottery.

⮕ If the floor plan is open, use one paint color throughout; preferably a light shade like Benjamin Moore's® "Sail Cloth" or Farrow & Ball's "Elephant's Breath," which has a hint of lilac. Use "Elephant's Breath" to create an edgy scheme that has warmth. Farrow & Ball's "Skimming Stone" and "Charleston" also make a nice combo of gray tones. You can always add contrasting color with the furnishings and artwork.

⮕ Keep your bathroom and kitchen streamlined. Look for clever storage solutions, whether it's under the sink, inside cupboards, or on a narrow shelf set around the room just a few inches down from the

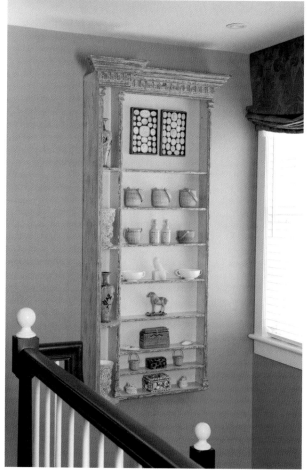

ceiling. Choose handmade, decorative, or creative containers for utilitarian items left in sight. Are you short on drawer space? Use a silver tea set or trophy cups to hold silverware on the counter.

➥ A vase of cut garden flowers is the loveliest accessory on any table. Think about this as you weed out the number of vases you own. I have a bad habit of keeping the vases that come with a bouquet from the florist. I never use them again, as the vases I own are nicer. Recycle these by either returning them to the florist or donating them to a thrift shop.

➥ An herb plant like lavender or a bowl of lemons or limes adds a fresh scent to the room. Use scented candles in a bathroom. It's the finishing touches that make a difference. Don't feel that every tabletop must be covered with items just because you have them.

➥ Try not to pile stuff on the floor. A small footstool or a child's chair is appealing when piled with books as part of your décor. A coffee table with a shelf underneath to hold magazines and newspapers helps keep the top free for displaying carefully selected, more attractive items.

OPPOSITE, LEFT:

The large coffee table with a shelf for holding newspapers and magazines underneath is attractive as well as practical.

OPPOSITE, RIGHT:

An architectural shelving unit from an old house is used as an interesting display piece for a collection of objects chosen for their shapes, sizes, and colors.

The two turquoise bottles deliberately challenge the neutral tones of the other items. This unit hangs on the wall at the top of the stairway, providing an interesting background for the display. "Consider empty space as important as the space filled with an object," the homeowner advises.

IDEAS FOR GETTING ORGANIZED

If you organize the items you use on a daily basis, you'll save the time and effort it takes to gather up these things when you need them. Here are a few suggestions to get you started.

1. Hang a bicycle basket on the back of your front door to hold keys, mail, suntan lotion, sunglasses, and all the things you bring in and take out on a regular basis.

2. If you entertain, clear one shelf or cupboard to hold all the things you need like napkins, placemats, and candles. Keep these items together in a basket that can be easily accessed.

3. Rearrange your spices and throw away all duplicates, "never will use," and expired items. A friend of mine even alphabetizes her spices!

4. Hang a row of hooks on the back of doors for coats and umbrellas. This will save space in your closet.

5. Give every family member his or her own basket for personal items that they usually dump on the kitchen counter, and have them find their own convenient place to keep it.

6. Look for unused wall space to hang a narrow bookcase. It doesn't have to hold books. The cubbies can be used for display or storage.

7. An all-white bedroom is restful and helps keep clutter at bay. When you bring anything colorful into a white room, it's jarring, and you will find an out-of-the-way place for it. It's easier than you might think to keep a white room free of clutter.

A retired woman bought a three-room cottage in Florida. "I retired early," she says, "and I was tired of Northern living. Since I have a passion for golf, I moved to Florida to take advantage of the weather." The little cottage is really two structures: a bedroom and bath in one and a living/dining/kitchen area in the other. These two structures are joined by a covered deck. "I love this place because it's unconventional," she explains, "and the deck is like a separate room that I use for different activities year-round. This room has an expandable teak table to accommodate more than four for a meal, and [I use it] as a workspace most of the time. It's wonderful to work outdoors with a view of the pool and vegetation. It's the size of an apartment, but I prefer the privacy of a house, and I like being able to putter outdoors even if my 'garden' is mostly in containers."

She enlisted the help of a decorator friend in town to put together a look that would be comfortable and easy to maintain, but with some surprises for her newly reinvented lifestyle. "I like to have friends over, but I do it spontaneously," she says. "Most of the time, I'm eating alone. I have cats. I didn't want the house to have the look of a lonely old lady who talks to her animals exclusively." This homeowner did not want to move into her new life with anything from the past. "Nothing fit and nothing went with the vibrant look of the South that I wanted," she reflects. "Besides, it would have been very expensive to move my furniture across the country, and none of it would have been appropriate for this cottage. You'd be surprised how much great stuff you can find online and from a really good furniture consignment shop."

She started by painting each room a different color—one blue, one green, and the other yellow—to create a completely different feeling in each one. The rooms are unified with bamboo furniture and vibrant artwork purchased locally. "Art usually reflects a region, so unless you have a really good or valuable collection that you're particularly attached to, I don't recommend moving it with you. It never seems to work in the new place if it's in a different part of the country," she observes.

TIP: It's easy to add a narrow shelf or molding above a doorway to use for displaying a collection of plates or simple found objects, like shells or starfish.

BELOW:
Bar stools around the kitchen island are perfect for the homeowner's meals alone or for serving drinks to guests. There's always a container filled with fresh oranges on the table, and the built-in window seat provides a great place for reading. The tropical fabric comes from a local sewing center, where she had the cushions custom-made. Starfish line all the windowsills and the ledge over the doorway.

2

LIVING IN STYLE

When furnishing a small living room, start with the basic pieces of upholstered furniture, such as a sofa and two comfortable chairs for a seating area. I have two love seats and two armless upholstered chairs in my living room. Each piece takes up less space than traditionally sized sofas and larger upholstered chairs with arms. It's easy to change the arrangement for different situations, because the furniture isn't too heavy to move. There's a coffee table between the love seats. If you want to try something different from a standard-size sofa and two upholstered chairs, consider a sectional sofa with perhaps one additional chair. It can provide all the seating you need.

Once you have the basic pieces, it's easy to add character with side tables, lamps, artwork, and window treatments. Try not to crowd all the furniture from your larger home into your new, smaller space just because you have it. Be selective. Determine what you need to buy to make your new home look as stylish as possible without sacrificing comfort.

Consider the way you like to entertain when planning the arrangement of furniture. If you have an outdoor deck or patio, use this to extend your living space when weather permits. Chairs from other areas, such as those in the dining room, can be pulled into service when you entertain. An ottoman is another item that can double as a coffee table as well as extra seating. Sometimes you might have to change how you entertain because of limited space. For example, intimate dinners for a

OPPOSITE:

An all-white palette benefits from a rich, colorful rug. It provides texture and introduces an understated vibrancy. This rug grounds the furnishings.

TIP: Small space does not limit you to small pieces of furniture. Anchor a small room with a large, comfortable sofa for ample seating. Add a couple of armless chairs and a coffee table. Concentrate on making the sofa the main attraction with down-filled cushions in lovely fabrics of contrasting texture, prints, and colors. The cushions should be comfy enough to sink into.

few might replace the big holiday parties you held in your larger home. Many people who changed their lifestyles in this way were surprised to find that entertaining in their smaller spaces was more satisfying than entertaining in their larger ones.

START WITH A COLOR SCHEME

Often a favorite color, or the colors in a painting, will dictate how a room is furnished. In the case of one homeowner, it started when he found a set of green folk-art chairs. "I love their used look," he says, "with the peeling paint and aqua color." Starting there, he stumbled on a "kitsch" *objet d'art*, a row of glass birds in shades of soft green and yellow. A white corner cabinet was a piece of furniture that survived the process of elimination during the move. He simply couldn't part with it, believing that it was not only attractive, but practical. All it took was a coat of lime green paint on the inside to show off his collection of milk glass and a variety of chinaware that he puts to good use when entertaining. Glass hurricane lanterns hold green candles, and the green bowl (found in a discount store) with delicate orchid plants completes a dining alcove. Whatever your favorite color, the one that makes you happiest is a great beginning.

OPPOSITE:
A sectional sofa is a good choice to maximize seating in a small room.

BELOW:
A sofa and two chairs would overwhelm this small living room. Built-in sofas with upholstered mattresses and bolsters created ample seating. The house has only one bedroom, so when the owners' two grown sons visit, the sofas are used for sleeping. This is better than a convertible sofa, as it doesn't require moving furniture or giving up floor space.

TIP: Color is an easy thing to change when you suddenly want to perk up a room.

Choosing Paint Colors with an Artist's Eye

The paint color of a room is often the first thing one notices. Paint is also an easy and inexpensive way to add color and drama. Color sets the mood. For example, a dark color often creates a cozy, cocoon-like feeling. A light color expands the feeling of a small room, and a powder room painted coral can be an unexpected surprise.

⮕ For a bedroom furnished with soft muted colors, Benjamin Moore suggests a deep, warm, sophisticated taupe to create an almost monochromatic color scheme that is far more interesting than a shade of white.

⮕ Neutral color schemes are always a safe choice, but to add a bit of drama, paint the walls in a soft sandy gray. It's considered warm with a rosy undertone, providing a noncompeting backdrop for any style of furnishings.

⮕ If you're comfortable using neutral colors throughout your home, Benjamin Moore offers a few suggestions for colors that work together: (a) "Barley," "Stone House," and "Providence Olive"; (b) "Carrington Beige," "Shaker Beige," and "Nantucket Gray"; and (c) "Manchester Tan," "Monroe Bisque," and "Camouflage." These are all elegant, subtle, and easy-to-live-with neutral shades that are more interesting than white or ivory.

⮕ My all-time favorite color is Farrow & Ball, "Mole's Breath." This gray is perfect for woodwork, ceilings, or a piece of furniture. It proves that a neutral interior is far from bland. I cannot imagine another paint-color name so thought-provoking. Farrow & Ball holds a contest every year for naming new paints, and they are worth checking out for the fun of it (us.farrow-ball.com).

OPPOSITE:

A color is a good beginning for a design theme in a room. The homeowner found the pair of green folk-art chairs and then painted the inside of a corner cabinet in lime green. The little birds started him on a search for more kitsch collectibles.

FOR COLOR IDEAS

LOOK TO THE FURNISHINGS AND OTHER ROOM ELEMENTS FOR INSPIRATION AND CHOOSE A COMPLEMENTARY OR CONTRASTING COLOR.

KITSCH IS KOOL!

Of German origin, the word *kitsch* came into use in the nineteenth century and has been used to categorize art that is considered to be a tasteless copy of an existing style. It was originally associated with art that is sentimental. Today, garden gnomes and other lawn ornaments are often considered kitschy. Such items, while looked down upon by serious art collectors, are highly desirable among retro collectors. And they always signal that a "not-so-serious person lives here."

17

THE FIFTH WALL

Designers call the ceiling the "fifth wall" to note its importance when choosing a color palette for a room. The ceiling is probably the largest expanse of uninterrupted space in a room, so its color greatly impacts its ambience. If you want to refresh a room instantly without completely repainting, look up. Paint the ceiling a contrasting color. My artist friend likes to keep the ceilings the same color throughout the house, no matter what color is used on the walls.

1 In rooms with neutral-colored walls, an unexpected pop of color on the ceiling can add an element of surprise and personality. It may sound a bit out of the ordinary, but a ceiling painted in a warm, subtle orange tone adds an overall glow to a room. It complements a wide range of other colors, making it a perfect choice to repeat throughout a home. Choose a lighter shade than the one you pick from the sample chip, and try it out before committing to a final color.

2 Choose paint specifically made for ceilings, such as Benjamin Moore's Waterborne Ceiling Paint. Its ultra-flat finish absorbs more light than flat wall paint, eliminating ceiling glare and hiding common surface imperfections. It's virtually flawless.

3 A large room with a high ceiling can feel impersonal. In this case, experiment with a ceiling color in a deeper shade than the walls. A darker tone of gray on a high ceiling brings the eye down, allowing the room's architectural details, such as molding or exposed beams, to take center stage. "Chelsea Gray" from Benjamin Moore is a rich and classic color.

4 If you've decorated with blue and white furnishings, consider white with a hint of blue for the ceiling. "It seems to lift the entire room," say the paint experts I interviewed at Benjamin Moore. "Subtle and sophisticated, it complements light-colored furnishings and can also soften a room with dark, traditional furniture."

LIGHTING: AN IMPORTANT ELEMENT OF DESIGN

Lighting can change the look of a room, yet its importance is often overlooked. When you are short of space, lighting choices become as important as the furniture. For example, floor lamps or uplights that sit on the floor are good for areas where you don't have room for a table on which to place a table lamp. If your space is too tight for even a floor lamp, then overhead lighting, which is usually preferred for kitchens, can be used in living and dining rooms. A swing-arm lamp is another good space-saving solution for living rooms as well as bedsides, because they are mounted on walls. They come in a variety of modern and traditional styles with a wide selection of shades. Recessed ceiling lights are often found in modern homes as well.

I always recommend dimmers on all lights so that you can set the lighting depending on how the room will be used and so that it will be at the correct setting every time you turn on the lights. The lighting in an eating area, for example, should be bright enough to see the food and people in the room without being overly bright or too dim. Not all homes achieve this, but it makes the evening more enjoyable when the lighting is just right. After the first impression, you should become so comfortable in a space that you no longer pay attention to the lighting and can enjoy the company you are with.

Chandeliers

I am totally attracted to chandeliers, especially when they appear in unexpected places like the kitchen and bathroom. If you are moving into an older home with new and improved bathrooms, there is nothing more exquisite than an ornate crystal chandelier for a lighting fixture. It can relieve the starkness of a sleek modern look and infuse a room with a touch of decadence.

OPPOSITE:
In this bedroom, the dark-blue ceiling helps the crown molding above the wardrobe units and windows stand out.

ABOVE:
Choose a lamp that has the right lighting, shape, and quality of design for the room and the task. This is an important element when furnishing a room.

LAMPS ARE IMPORTANT ACCESSORIES.

GOOD LAMPS, WHETHER NEW OR ANTIQUE, ARE WORTH SPENDING MONEY ON. SCRIMP ON OTHER STUFF IF YOU MUST. NO ONE WILL KNOW THE SIDE TABLE DOESN'T HAVE A PEDIGREE, BUT A WELL-DESIGNED LAMP SPEAKS VOLUMES.

Table Lamps

Table lamps serve more purpose than just providing light for specific tasks. In fact, in the world of interior design, they are considered an important decorating accessory. Their soft lighting is important for creating ambience. If your old lamps don't look good in your new space and you can't afford to replace them, consider new shades to update your lamps. One lamp that never seems to go out of style is the classic candlestick lamp. It is perfect for bedrooms in particular because it comes in different heights for bedside reading. These lamps are often chosen for a casual decorating style, and with their slim shapes, they take up minimal space when placed on a table.

DANISH MODERN: A GOOD CHOICE

Danish modern or mid-century modern furniture is light in style and therefore a good choice for making a small living room feel airy. An architect and his partner, a real-estate agent, downsized to a ground-level, modern, modest one-bedroom condominium. There's a living room with an open kitchen at one end and a bedroom and bath on

NOTE: One wall is painted a darker shade of linen, providing a subtle change as the natural light varies at different times of the day and year.

the second floor. The floors are joined by a modern, circular staircase. "We especially like the balcony off our bedroom," they point out. There was a screened-in porch off the living room that they enclosed and made into a small sitting area with built-in sofas. The sofas are deep enough to use for an occasional overnight guest, and for privacy they added doors in the living room. They wallpapered with a distinctly contrasting color and a pattern that works with their decorating style. "We had a lot of fun furnishing this place," they say. "Because we knew the style of furnishings we wanted, it was easy to narrow our focus."

They first made a floor plan and determined the basic seating arrangement and what pieces they needed for comfortable living. They recall, "At first, we weren't thinking about having others in our home. We were just thinking of our own comfort." Once they had lived in the condo for a few months, they realized that a separate dining area was a necessity. To that end, they covered a small outdoor patio area with a bamboo structure and built seating around a small table. "It only works in good weather," they explain, "but the climate is pretty good for eight months of the year. When it gets cooler, we entertain with luncheons rather than dinners."

OPPOSITE:

Subtle colors are used for the upholstered furniture with excitement from the artwork. Lacking storage, one large cabinet is filled with shelves and drawers and offers height to break up the expanse of light-colored walls.

BELOW:

Many people want a workstation in their homes. Designate a work space at one end of a room with a simple desk. Add a chair and inexpensive bookcases placed on either side of the desk.

FOUND SPACES

When space is at a premium, you want to find ways to utilize that little unused corner that might have been overlooked. For example, a narrow wall might be the perfect spot for a shelving unit to hold books. Or a desk might fit into that space under a stairway for a home office.

Repurposing space in your downsized home gives you the opportunity to make it over to suit your needs. When you downsize, you don't necessarily have to use the space as it was originally intended. You might find a cozy little three-bedroom house but need only two bedrooms. Consider turning that third bedroom into a good-size second bathroom or taking out a wall to enlarge an adjoining room. For example, in addition to adding a new bathroom, a homeowner in Napa Valley removed one wall of a bedroom to enlarge the living area, adding a sliding barn-style door on a track that turns the space back into a bedroom when she has an occasional guest. This was the second phase of her renovation.

OPPOSITE:

A small area under a sloped ceiling was perfect for a desk and display of art. The folk-art table, chair, and small cabinet were antique-shop finds.

RIGHT:

A second bedroom and bath were created in unfinished attic space. The circular staircase from the first floor adds a beautifully sculptural presence that is seen from the living room.

The owner of a one-bedroom, 800-square-foot (79-square-meter) urban apartment needed a separate dining room for entertaining.

Roughan Interior Design took space from the living room and created an ebony screen as a partial divider wall. The space was well-utilized.

Draperies hung almost at the ceiling make this living room look grander and the window expanse larger. A frosted-glass partition divides the room in this studio apartment to create separate spaces.

The living-room side of the half-wall partition allows light to pass through, thus maintaining the open, airy feel of the apartment.

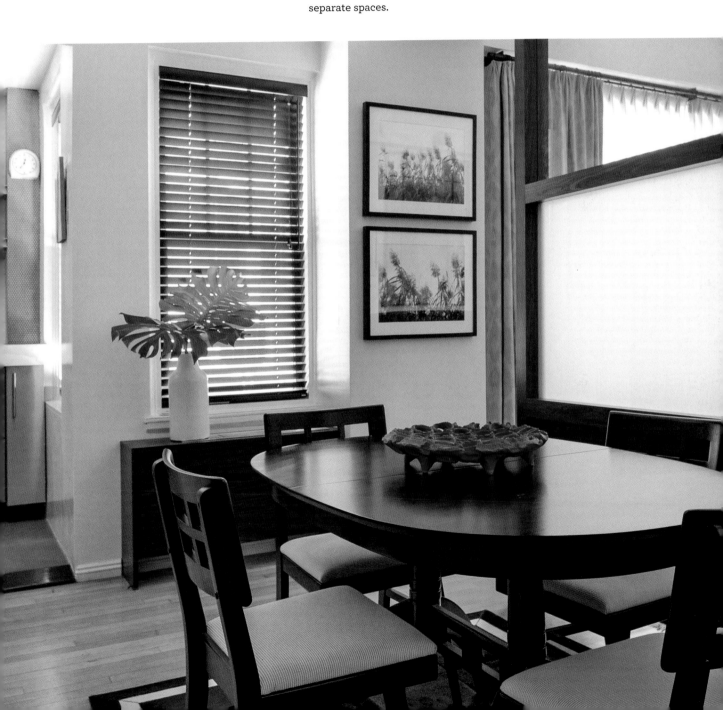

Window Seats

Window seats are wonderful areas for creating extra seating or a cozy spot for reading. If you have a niche, a bay-window area, or room to create a space for a window seat, they're easy to build. Add an upholstered cushion and some throw pillows. Another option is to leave the area open underneath for a bookshelf, or to have doors installed under the seat for storage. Some window seats are built so that the seats are hinged at the back and can be lifted for storing large items. One homeowner custom-built a banquette for a dining area (see page 148) for storing large kitchen trays and small appliances, like a mixer and blender that are only used occasionally.

OPPOSITE, ABOVE:
The homeowner wanted the perfect spot to unwind and built a window seat at the top of the stairs on the landing. Look for areas like this to add comfort and interest to your home. This is an easy and inexpensive project that can provide storage under the seat as well.

OPPOSITE, BELOW:
A bay window provides the perfect place for a window seat. Some homeowners place a tea table (which is higher than a coffee table) in front of a window seat to use as a dining area. With this setup, chairs are only needed on one side when serving a meal.

ABOVE:
A window seat in a bedroom provides drawer space and is luxuriously upholstered with the same fabric as the window treatment and barrel love seat. The fabric unifies the room. Swing-arm wall lights are convenient for reading.

LEFT:

The interior of a beach house is expanded visually with the use of white paint on the walls and ceiling. A built-in window seat provides a substitute for a sofa, and the addition of two ample armchairs creates a compact seating area. White sailcloth slipcovers are a practical choice for casual living.

29

Finding Storage in Unlikely Places

Everyday items from the past make great accessories *and* provide storage space. For example, a collection of old boxes that has been used as storage since early American times not only lends character to shelves or a desktop but is also handy.

Make an entryway work with one large piece like a weathered trunk that stores bulky items and serves as a bench or a display for a large basket of flowers. A clothes tree or hooks on the wall and an umbrella stand can complete a vignette. A patterned rug or painted floor is an interesting finishing touch.

RIGHT:

To save space, interior designer Christina Roughan of Roughan Interior Design used under-the-counter, high-end appliances and open shelves in an urban apartment. The bright-colored pots pop out against the white tiled background and infuse the space with a bit of surprise.

OPPOSITE:

Sliding barn doors on a track are easy to install. They take up much less space than a standard door on hinges that swings in or out.

GOOD QUALITY AND CLASSIC DESIGN

WILL NEVER

GO OUT OF STYLE.

TIP: Sliding barn doors save space
and are architecturally interesting.
You can browse a wide selection
on Real Sliding Hardware's website
(realslidinghardware.com).

EVALUATE AND REEVALUATE

EVERY SINGLE PIECE YOU OWN,
THEN EDIT CAREFULLY, AND THEN AGAIN,
UNTIL YOU'VE CREATED AN
ARTFULLY LAYERED LOOK.

ADJUST

THE WAY YOU ENTERTAIN
ACCORDING TO YOUR SPACE.
COMPROMISE CAN LEAD TO
CREATIVE CHANGES.

KEEP AN OPEN MIND

IF YOUR TASTE IN FURNISHINGS
IS BEYOND YOUR BUDGET. THE
TRICK TO THRIFT-SHOP DECORATING
IS MIXING THE BARGAINS WITH
GOOD ACCESSORIES.

IT'S AN ART

TO CHOOSE THINGS WELL
RATHER THAN OFTEN.

Underused space can often be found under a stairway. Pegs on the wall hold hats, and fishing gear fills an old barrel. A basket on the floor stores dried flowers, flip-flops, or mittens, depending on the season.

33

ARRANGED FOR COMFORT

A woman who lives alone sold her family's large home and moved into a narrow one-room townhouse. She likes living surrounded by her collections but says she has to contain them. Most important to her was creating a comfortable sitting area in the small living-room space. She kept two comfortable chairs and a sofa from her larger home because they were high quality and expensive to replace. Using a shabby chic approach, she had slipcovers made in white sailcloth and added small floral-printed throw pillows and not much else. "I live alone," she points out, "but when I occasionally entertain I just pull over a few chairs from the dining table." She adds, "I love sitting here, where I can see every part of the house. This house feels spacious because of the light colors and high ceiling, and it has a slouchy, comfy feel that puts everyone at ease—mostly me."

When downsizing, one homeowner created a feminine corner in the living room with her favorite china pieces. She artfully arranged them on a lovely painted tray table that has moved with her several times over many years. "I always have fresh flowers on that table," she says.

It only takes three good upholstered pieces—two club chairs and a full-size sofa—to create a sitting area. Throw pillows are easy and inexpensive to change when you want to try out new colors.

Small round tables are practical in this apartment living room. They can be moved around depending on the situation. A fresh bouquet of white flowers is perfect in this elegantly soft colored room.

TIP: Pick the right size coffee table. To ensure visual balance, choose a coffee table that is two-thirds the length of your sofa. When it comes to height, the top of the table should be level with the middle of the sofa seat cushion.

UPSCALE DOWNSIZING

EMBRACING SMALLNESS

An architect friend who had experience designing wooden sailboats for Hinckley Yachts in Maine designed my house. Since we live on an island, my husband and I wanted a small, cozy den that would have the feel—and the same size—of a cabin on a boat. The room is only 8 × 9 feet (2.4 × 2.7 meters) with built-in sofas and narrow shelves running along the walls. There is a corner fireplace to the left of the opening, and to the right is an armoire that houses the television set and drawers for storage. The room is wired for sound, and when we're in this space on a cold winter night and the fire is roaring, there's no place we'd rather be. It is, admittedly, a room for only two. If we have a guest, we sit in the living room, as the den is too tight for comfort. We rather like this selfish little room.

A small room requires an organized plan for use. The top shelf is just wide enough to hold selected books, and the shelf under it is quite narrow, just wide enough for the ever-changing photographs of our family. (I try to limit family photographs to personal rooms like this den and the bedroom.) We deliberately made the room this small after living in a very large house with a den three times this size. In the winter, we were always dragging our chairs closer to the fireplace, so we decided we wanted a room with seating that was always close enough to the fireplace to be comfortably warm. And that's what this turned out to be. We spent a lot of time measuring and

TIP: To make a small room feel cozy, everything you choose should be in scale with the size of the room. Narrow shelves spanning a room can provide display areas for photographs and knickknacks. If something doesn't feel right, remove it. Keep perfecting the space by adding and taking away items.

determining the dimensions of the room. I know many people would be tempted, while building, to make a room larger. Most people think they need more space than they actually do, but everyone who experiences this room never wants to leave. The ceiling is low, which adds to its cocoon-like feeling. The room wraps its arms around you. The fireplace wall, on an angle toward the sofas, is made of small, worn pink bricks that I retrieved from a salvage yard. They came from the demolition of a chimney on a house built in the early 1800s. The hearth in front of the fireplace is made of the same brick. Every detail in this room was planned, including the use of small-table and overhead lighting to avoid floor lamps. The two windows pull out from the top to open, and folding shutters on each side block out light when desired.

OPPOSITE:

A small 8 × 9–foot (2.4 × 2.7–meter) cocoon-like room was created with everything built in.

3

DINING IN STYLE

Few small houses or apartments have separate dining rooms. If there isn't a separate dining room or obvious area for dining in your smaller space, it can be fun to approach carving out space elsewhere for dining as a creative challenge. First, you'll want to find room for everyday meals, depending on how many people are in your family. Next, think about how you like to entertain. Remember, you may have to change the way you did this when you had a large home. For example, if you had sit-down dinners for eight or ten, you might have to consider buffet-style dinners or more intimate dinners with four or six guests.

INVENTIVE EATING SPACES

Most families today have space in the kitchen for eating, whether it's on stools at an island or a table and chairs at one end of the kitchen. For a more formal approach, a dining area is often created at one end of the living room. You might create a visual separation by placing a large piece of furniture, such as a china cabinet, between the living room and dining area. Another way to visually separate living and dining areas is with paint. Choose two different shades of the same paint color for the two areas. A hanging chandelier over a dining table can also visually delineate the dining area from the living room.

OPPOSITE:
The soft green walls in the dining room create an elegant background with bright white trim. Accents of green are used on the fabric, lampshades, and place mats. Live plants are added throughout the room. The wall color is "Churlish Green" from Farrow & Ball.

Many homeowners with large families like to have family dinners or make room for entertaining for special occasions. In a smaller space, you have to consider this in a practical way. You don't want an oversize table taking up space when you only occasionally need room for eight or more. A drop-leaf table or a table with a leaf extension can accommodate extra guests when needed. Light pull-up chairs might be used in the living room most of the time. Sometimes the shape of the table is important. A round table, for example, is often more practical than one with sharp corners. Round or oval tables often fit more gracefully into small

OPPOSITE:

A homeowner with a large extended family bought a small cottage that lacked a dining area. There was, however, a lovely screened-in porch off the living room. She removed a wall and was able to renovate and create a space to fit a table and chairs that works for family gatherings. This room has almost doubled her living space.

RIGHT, ABOVE:

The homeowner created a small eating area at one end of the kitchen with found materials. The base of the table is made from repurposed wood and the top is a slab of marble cut to size. It extends slightly at one end to make room for a fifth place setting when needed.

RIGHT, BELOW:

A narrow kitchen in an apartment had little space for a dining table. The owners added a drop-down table with a gracefully curved front to save space when not in use. To fit a brown and white color scheme, the secondhand wooden dining chairs were painted white and covered in a plush chocolate brown fabric.

areas. A drop-leaf table can be placed against a wall to hold lamps and an arrangement of flowers. Pull up the front leaf for dining alone or when you have one guest. A bench under the table is a good way to seat people on one side when the table is fully open. It's easier to store a bench under the table, for example, than a few extra chairs. Fold-up chairs are good for deskwork and around a kitchen or dining table. They can be stored in the back of a closet when not in use.

BELOW:
A mirror acts as a visual divider between the living and eating areas of one large space. A tall plant breaks up the wall expanse in the corner of the room, whereas a piece of furniture would make the corner feel too heavy.

OPPOSITE:
A single man downsized to a one-bedroom cottage and created a delightful dining area for one, where he enjoys meals with a view from his living-room window. He says, "When a friend comes for dinner, there's room for two but no more." The vase of flowers is removed when there are dinner guests.

TIP: Even when dining in the kitchen, use candlelight and set an elegant table.

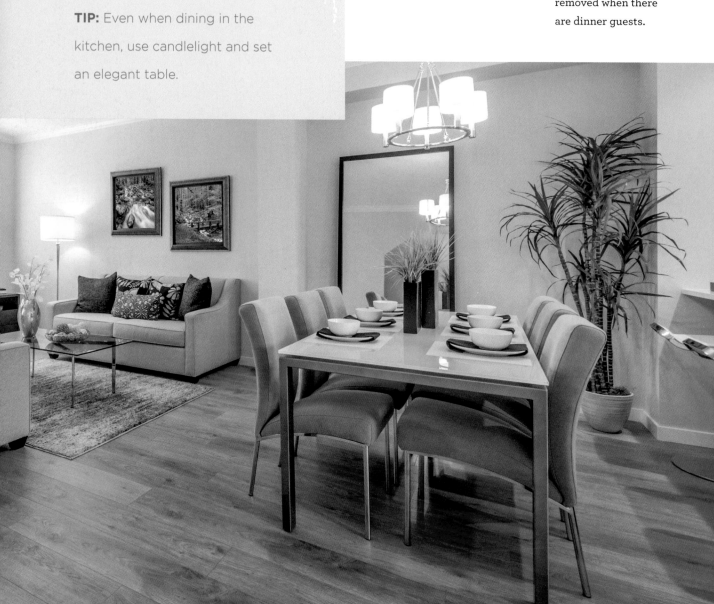

CREATIVE TABLE SETTINGS

Just because you've downsized does not mean that you have to pare down when it comes to entertaining beautifully. Many people find it most difficult to get rid of the china that they've collected or inherited over the years. I love dishes. I've been collecting them for years, in all different colors for different seasons and occasions. I simply can't resist adding to what I have, which is way too much to use in a lifetime. I love setting a table in creative ways and always use my ornate silverware (some were wedding gifts, some from my grandmother), even when I'm setting a table for a barbecue on the deck.

TIP: Great items to buy on a vacation are napkins or place mats. They're light, easy to pack, and remind you of your trip each time you use them.

RIGHT:

Short on space, the homeowners created an eating area in a hallway. For practically no money, they created a counter by installing a hollow-core, white-stained door on fold-down piano hinges, with 2 × 3–inch (5 × 7–cm) wooden posts for supports. The door folds flat against the wall when not in use. The curtains are made from dish towels to match the checkerboard floor and hang simply on tension rods with clip-on curtain rings. No sewing is involved! The stools (from Walmart) were painted white, but the homeowner coated the tops with glossy, red Krylon® spray paint.

It somehow makes a meal seem special, and I like my guests to feel they are being celebrated.

Fresh flowers are always an easy way to create a centerpiece, but I also like to use fresh seasonal vegetables, like gourds and pumpkins. Shells make a table interesting in the summer. My husband and I eat breakfast at our kitchen-island counter, and the first thing I do, even before turning on the

ABOVE:

The yellow walls in this dining room set the theme for the table setting. The homeowner is an interior decorator and always sets a table with flowers. Plates, place mats, napkins with navy-blue accents, and a grosgrain ribbon make the table festive for spring.

TIP: Polish good silverware twice a year, and, if not used every day, store it in a flannel-lined silverware box. Add a piece of chalk, mothball, or dryer sheet to fight tarnishing.

OPPOSITE:
Silver trophy cups provide a creative and practical way to hold silverware when you're short on drawer space.

LEFT:
Every table deserves a bouquet of freshly cut flowers. A renowned florist and stylist says, "Use what's in your garden for a casual but lovely bouquet."

coffee maker, is put out the placemats and cloth napkins (never paper)! I bought wonderful French country napkins in a shop in Calistoga, California, on a recent trip (along with the wonderful coffee mugs from the diner next door), and every morning we are reminded of that trip. It's a little bonus. So, no matter how small your dining table or counter area, dress it up with an interesting table setting.

BELOW: Decorative Indian corn, bright-orange cloth napkins, miniature white pumpkins, and vibrant flowers create a table setting ideal for autumn.

OPPOSITE: Layered plates, each with a different pattern but in the same color, create a more interesting table setting than one where everything matches. This homeowner says, "I always use napkin rings. It's such an easy way to add glam to the table."

TIP: If you don't have a garden, begin a habit of including flowers on your grocery shopping list.

4

KITCHENS AND BATHS REDESIGNED

Kitchens and bathrooms are the first rooms—sometimes the *only* rooms—that need renovation. In a small house, they can be given the full upscale treatment, even if your style is retro. Everyone wants them to function at top level for maximum efficiency.

DREAM KITCHENS

Renovation is an opportunity to use high-end fixtures and appliances that are now being offered for small kitchens. For example, often associated with industrial or restaurant use, a Wolf®, or Viking®, range and oven have always been favored by those who love to cook. Now, these gas ranges are available in more compact sizes to fit into apartments and small kitchens.

Another area for high-profile design is in the hardware you choose. Even if you aren't renovating, your kitchen could probably use a little upgrade. The simplest and most cost-efficient way to do this is to add new cabinet pulls and faucet set for the sink. Some homeowners go further and replace the cabinet doors without replacing the entire unit. Others even remove their cabinet doors in favor of open shelves to lighten up the space. One homeowner not only removed the doors but also lined the cabinets completely with wallpaper that matched her taste and the style of the house.

OPPOSITE:
The homeowner painted everything in the open kitchen white and added new appliances, industrial lamps, and white tile backsplash.

A tired kitchen was revived with gray paint, new cabinet hardware, and fixtures. A shelf between cabinets holds chinaware, but more shelves could be added for more storage or for holding a collection of kitchen items like glasses, bowls, or mugs.

A minimalist planned a small kitchen that opens to the living room in a city loft apartment. Everything is hidden behind doors, including small appliances. Know how much time and energy you want to spend on maintenance before planning such a kitchen.

While it's often a good idea to invest in upgrades, there are a few features that are worth keeping. For example, the deep porcelain sinks found in early American farmhouses are coming back in style in modern kitchens. If your kitchen has older features that look great and function well, it might make sense to leave them where they are.

If you're interested in a retro look for your kitchen, vintage and vintage-inspired appliances generally have smaller footprints than modern-day, giant family-size refrigerators, oven ranges, and dishwashers. They can also add decorative charm and a welcome pop of color to a small space. (Aqua appliances were popular because the color seemed modern when they first appeared in the 1950s.) You can find vintage appliances in home catalogs and online. Reproductions often work better and have the same charming retro look as original appliances.

OPPOSITE:
Gray paint was used on one wall of a kitchen to create a dramatic background for everyday chinaware neatly displayed on narrow shelves.

RIGHT, ABOVE:
For a country kitchen, edge the front of the shelves with paper doily trim. It comes in rolls where kitchen supplies are sold.

RIGHT, BELOW:
One little cabinet is crammed with the homeowner's cherished cups and saucers, with pitchers and bowls above. While this collection is a jumble of items, the objects still look interesting and are used all the time. The cabinet takes up minimal space.

RIGHT:

This renovated kitchen has a deep porcelain sink and cabinets painted in a soft butterscotch color that is typical in older homes. Consider this color for adding warmth to a modern kitchen.

TIP: When creating dining space in the kitchen, decidedly comfortable dining chairs will make the area look and feel less like a kitchen and more like a dining room. Consider also adding a chandelier or modern light fixture.

The kitchen, which is open to the living room, makes up the first floor of this Southern home. To create a casual eating and kitchen prep area, the homeowners built an island with funky swing-out tractor seats. A little outdoor space off the kitchen has a table for four, which they use year-round.

The island in this modern streamlined galley kitchen is used for every meal. Interior designer Elizabeth Winship covered the bar chairs with fun fabric from Nantucket Looms to give the area a "dressed-up" look for casual dining.

TIP: If you're dining in the kitchen, be sure to install dimmers on the lights.

RIGHT, ABOVE:

A new sink and upscale faucet, as well as interesting subway tiles, instantly upgraded this kitchen.

RIGHT, BELOW:

A deep porcelain sink adds farmhouse style to a newly built kitchen designed by Elizabeth Winship.

OPPOSITE, ABOVE:

In this kitchen/ dining/living- room combination, yam-colored walls are outstandingly cheerful. "I moved from the North to the South and wanted my downsized home to reflect the sunny weather," said the homeowner. The color of spices also influenced the color choices in each room of the house. The opposite wall, which is part of the living room, is cinnamon colored.

OPPOSITE, BELOW:

A minimal galley kitchen was created on one wall. To add character, the homeowner used painted white shiplap on the walls and cut thick, weathered boards salvaged from a construction site for the shelves. Small under-counter "puck" lights were hardwired under the bottom shelf. (These lights are available online or from home centers like Lowe's and Home Depot. They're also available as plug-ins.)

ABOVE:

An old kitchen was renovated with a deep stainless steel sink, new fixtures, and marble countertops. Since the kitchen was small, it was relatively inexpensive to upgrade with quality products.

RIGHT:

A small, well-planned kitchen can be extremely efficient. This homeowner used the services of a kitchen outfitter and was able to personalize it with her art and collectibles.

BEST SMALL BATHROOMS EVER!

Bathrooms are probably used as often as kitchens, and they *must* function well—no question about it. When you downsized in square footage, you may have forfeited a lovely big bathroom for one that's half the size. *I cannot possibly make this bathroom work* might be your first thought. *Where will I put all my cosmetics, let alone towels, extra toilet paper, medicines, and the cleaning supplies I had room for in my former bathrooms?*

Believe it or not, there *is* storage space in even the tiniest bathroom, though it may not be obvious. If you're shaking your head and insistently saying "No! You haven't seen my bathroom," then you'll be happy to know that you haven't begun to really look at every square inch to see how it might be used for a shelf or storage unit. There are so many ways to create more space simply by looking at the room objectively. No negative emotions are allowed! Become the consultant called in to make that bathroom work, no matter what you say to dissuade yourself. Just know this: Failure is not an option. And it will look sensational.

RIGHT:

A couple removed a single sink unit and replaced it with a cabinet and two sinks. Everything, including towels, is stored underneath. Two mirrors and good lighting make this room efficient for two.

TIP: Vintage claw-foot tubs were often made from heavy cast iron. Today, you can find reproductions of claw-foot tubs made from molded plastic. These plastic claw-foot tubs are much lighter and easier to install.

OPPOSITE:
A modern bathroom was a luxury at the top of the homeowner's list when he began renovating his one-bedroom ranch-style home.

RIGHT:
Attic space was renovated to create a guest bedroom and bath. A claw-foot tub is graceful and deep. It's perfect for an older home or for achieving a retro look in a modern bathroom.

OPPOSITE:

The cottage feel
of this bathroom
was embraced and
exaggerated with
pink-and-white-
striped wallpaper and
a new pedestal sink.
The claw-foot tub is
original to the house;
and with no linen
closet, an antique
table is perfect for
holding extra towels.

ABOVE:

A tiny space under
a staircase was used
to create a first-floor
powder room. The
elegant wallpaper,
light fixture, and
tiniest corner sink are
a complete surprise
when guests use
this room.

CREATE AN ILLUSION OF SPACE

THE FOLLOWING TIPS WILL HELP CREATE THE ILLUSION OF MORE SPACE IN A SMALL BATHROOM.

1. Create a horizontal line around the room with a chair rail on the wall, midway between the floor and ceiling. You can buy the wood for the rail at a lumberyard and easily install it yourself.

2. Paint colors can be used to create a feeling of space. For example, if you choose a slate-gray color for the walls, paint the ceiling in a slightly lighter shade of the same color.

3. If there is no window, create a "view" with a tile pattern, mirror, or scenic wallpaper on just one wall.

4. With the space underneath, a claw-foot tub gives the illusion of floating and seems to take up less space than a built-in tub. Their shape is graceful, and the depth makes them marvelous for soaking. They also add elegance to a modern or not-so-new bathroom.

5. A mirrored wall expands the space; but another, perhaps more interesting, treatment is to create an arrangement of different-size mirrors with a variety of frames on one wall.

6. If there's a window in the room, hang a mirror on the opposite wall to reflect light and the view from the window. Down lights also make walls seem to recede by washing them with light.

7. If you are tiling the floor, use large floor tiles so there are fewer grout lines to break up the room. Laying the tile on the diagonal also visually lengthens the room.

REPURPOSING SPACE

A woman bought a small three-bedroom, one-bath home in the Napa Valley area of California. "It felt very cramped, with low ceilings and very small rooms," she said. A decorator friend suggested turning the smallest bedroom into a second bathroom. The new bathroom would be spacious and have a door leading to the master bedroom. Plus, she would still have an extra bedroom for guests and for use as an office. She wanted to keep the rustic charm of the house but updated the bathroom by sanding and refinishing the existing wood floors, adding beadboard to the walls, and installing the shower, sink, and toilet in a retro style. A weathered barrel is used to hold extra towels, and she installed pegs for holding towels.

BELOW:
A small bedroom was turned into a luxurious bathroom.

OPPOSITE:
A closet was repurposed for a small bathroom in a seaside cottage. Beadboard on the walls is painted glossy white. The brown granite sink-surround is a nice contrast to the stark white interior. All accessories have a marine theme. For example, the blue towels and mirror give a nod to the sea. Note the space-saving all-in-one faucet/handle unit.

SENSATIONALLY SMALL

When I was first married, my first home had a bathroom so impossibly small that I had to sit sideways on the toilet. To get into the room and close the door, I had to suck in my stomach. I was determined to make that tiny bathroom the most functional *and* glamorous room in the house. Besides, a bathroom should make you feel good when you stand in front of the mirror every day before going to work.

There's not much you can do with the layout of a tiny bathroom unless you're doing major renovation, so work with what you have. Rather than dwelling on the size of your bathroom, think, *How can I make it exquisitely wonderful?* I know I say it often, but keep reminding yourself to embrace its size and make it an asset.

My husband and I had scratched together just enough money to buy our first home. There was barely a nickel for much more than ingenious decorating. The trick was to make the room seem bigger using what was already in place. While I wasn't trained as a decorator (writing about design is different than actually doing it), I was raised in a do-it-yourself family. It was a family of creative people, from my mother, a fashion designer's assistant, to my grandfather, who was an architect. Approaching everything in my life from an "I can do it" point of view comes naturally to me, so a bathroom, I figured, was a no-brainer. (When I got to the kitchen, things didn't go as well, but mistakes are learning experiences.)

The room not only was small but also lacked a window. This, as it turned out, would be its most appealing feature, as I was able to turn it into an elegant, cozy room that I ultimately enjoyed as my "time-out" place. When I shut the door, I shut out the world, and it became a very safe, quiet retreat whenever I needed an escape from "noise." It wrapped its arms around me and allowed me to feel undisturbed when I needed a moment to myself. How many places in your home have this quality?

CREATING STORAGE

If you're remodeling a similarly sized room, you can easily create built-in storage shelves by adding niches built into the wall between the studs. They will be about three inches (7.6 cm) deep. If you have mirrored glass, cut it to fit the entire shelf unit, including its sides, top, back, and bottom. It will give the illusion of space and provide adequate storage for everyday needs.

I've lived in many homes since, and in every one of them, I have always tried to re-create that feeling in one of the rooms, whether it's a niche, a corner, or my office space.

The first thing I did was to choose an adhesive wallpaper with a bold, all-over cabbage-rose pattern featuring big green leaves and a deep rose-colored background. (Self-adhesive wallpaper is easiest for a do-it-yourself project.) It was elegant and unexpected for a small room. I had never wallpapered before. Since the room was small, it didn't take much material, so the cost, even for quality paper, wasn't a consideration. If it had been, I would have chosen a rich paint color as an alternative. I wallpapered the walls *and* the ceiling. This was very important! By doing the whole room, I created a continuous design and set the tone for the ambience. Since the door was made of cheap, hollow-core thin plywood, I wallpapered right over it to finish the seamless look. If the door had been painted, it would have stood out like a big elephant in the room.

The second thing I did was change the lighting. There was an ugly light fixture on each side of a plain, unframed mirror over the sink. The room clearly needed more and better lighting. Overhead lighting is very unflattering in a bathroom. Avoid it at all costs. It is not good for self-esteem. I found a pair of good-looking sconces, and the electrician was able to place them at eye level on either side of the mirror. These lights provide illumination without casting shadows for the best lighting possible. I found a cheap but ornate picture frame at a yard sale to mount over the mirror.

Thirdly (and I know this might sound gross), I carpeted the tiny floor area with deep rose-colored, weather-resistant carpeting, making the whole room soundproof.

Fourthly, I looked for storage space, inch by inch. I hung a hotel-style chrome shelving unit over the toilet for towels. I used a basket under the small pedestal sink for toilet tissue, room freshener spray, and small bottles of cleaning supplies and outfitted the minute shower with a hanging caddy for shampoo and soap.

Finally, the icing on the cake was a board that I had cut to fit over the toilet tank and between the side walls. The board displayed items, including a framed photograph, a bowl of scented stones (or potpourri) to give the room a faint floral scent, and a few knickknacks that I loved. A small bathroom is a great place to create an art gallery because it's easy to fill and make interesting if you do it artfully. I framed four small botanical prints of roses and hung them in a square grouping on one wall between the sink and toilet, which was the only uninterrupted wall expanse. To finish off the look, I bought new rose-colored towels, beautiful pink bars of soap, and a lovely rosebud printed china cup for toothbrushes and toothpaste. All the cosmetics were contained in pretty containers. Nothing was makeshift in this little room, and I loved perfecting it, switching the knickknacks on the toilet shelf from time to time. It satisfied a desire to display collectibles, a few at a time.

RIGHT:

A renovation on a budget included adding a sink and Corian® counter that was cut to fit between two walls in a bathroom. To avoid spending more on custom cabinets, the homeowner simply affixed a curtain on a tension rod to create hidden storage space.

SMALL BUT ELEGANT

I have lived in many houses since my first one. Now, I have a small powder room just large enough for a sink and toilet. After many years of procrastination, I finally chose a paint color: a steel gray from Benjamin Moore.

It should be noted that I went through a stage of thinking coral would be a good color but was never able to commit to it. Then linen became the choice. While I tell my readers to be decisive, I am always the first to admit to my own insecurities and areas of procrastination. When I finally did commit to the right color, my daughter, who is far better at this than I, undertook the job of painting the room. It took a day. Prior to painting the walls and ceiling, she painted all the trim a glossy white.

The bathroom took two coats of water-based paint. When it was finished, I was thrilled. The walls of the powder room, which is used by guests, are a perfect gallery space for artwork, photographs, or anything that is interesting and framed. The wall over the sink and opposite the toilet makes the room feel more spacious than it is. On the walls perpendicular to the sink, I hung early black-and-white family photographs in black or white frames. They are reflected in a mirrored wall. On another wall, I have two of my handcrafted decoupage plates featuring calla lily prints. A tall vase on the toilet shelf holds an array of silk flowers to match. They look and feel amazingly real!

OPPOSITE:
Steel-gray walls create a background for an art gallery in a small powder room. A shelf from the top of a desk fits perfectly between the walls over the toilet tank.

RIGHT:
Embrace the smallness of a tiny bathroom and celebrate its size. Don't choose a light color. Go dark with gorgeous wallpaper and an antique sink unit. Choose art, a mirror, fixtures, and lighting with care. A linen towel and antique vase of wildflower sprigs make a powder room inviting.

TIP: When you only need a little of something, like wallpaper, make it extravagant. It will always be affordable and look sensational! This is not where you want to go budget.

5

BEDROOMS YOU'LL NEVER WANT TO LEAVE

The bedroom is my favorite room. It's where I go to relax. I keep it clutter-free, and its colors are soft and soothing. When filled with neutral colors and fabrics and minimally furnished, bedrooms provide a calming effect. I believe that a well-designed bedroom should be the place that restores you. On average, a third of your life is spent here. Spending money to create the perfect bedroom makes sense because it affects your well-being more than any other room in the house. Toward that end, the bed should be sumptuous and inviting. Creating the ideal space can be done in any size room. It's all about the choices of furniture, carpeting, window treatments, and especially the bedding.

Groucho Marx once said, "Anything that can't be done in bed isn't worth doing." I'm with him, but I'd go one step further and add: "But first and foremost, the bed must be made with freshly ironed sheets and pillowcases." Not everyone agrees with me, but I find that this small act of smoothing out the wrinkles (over which I have some control) makes the bed look and feel luxurious. I often take my sheets to a commercial laundry because it's an indulgence I can justify.

Once you know where you'll place the bed (and there may only be one option), a side table with at least one drawer will make all the difference between a pretty bedside

OPPOSITE:
Ceiling angles dictated the furniture layout in this bedroom. A built-in window seat has storage below. The soft seafoam color and old-world window valances make this room a good retreat at the end of the day. (See page 17 for "Choosing Paint Colors.")

arrangement and a utilitarian place for a pair of glasses, a phone, or other items that you want within reach. If you want a king-size bed but the room is more suited to a queen, consider a narrow shelf on each side of the bed to conserve space.

When hanging art over a bed, experts recommend positioning it three inches (7.6 cm) lower than you might think. It will look perfect. Next, think about sconces for lighting. Wall-mounted lighting won't take up precious space. Plus, if you hang them approximately a foot (30.5 cm) above your head, they make the ideal reading light.

BELOW:

A calm bedroom is a wonderful place for relaxation. Keep everything soft in color and simple in design.

OPPOSITE:

Three pieces of handcrafted furniture are perfectly suited to this simple Shaker-style room.

IN AN INTERVIEW, WELL-KNOWN INTERIOR DESIGNER VICENTE WOLF SAID, "PLACE THE BED SO THAT WHEN YOU COME INTO A BEDROOM, YOU SEE THIS MOST IMPOSING PIECE OF FURNITURE FROM THE FOOT TO GET THE FULL EFFECT."

UPSCALE DOWNSIZING

The bed is a little wide to fit between the windows of this small bedroom, but the homeowner wanted a queen-size bed and didn't want to sacrifice comfort. Neutral tones dominate the room.

The bedroom is barely large enough for a full-size bed, but the room functions well and has a cozy cottage feeling. Swing arm lamps are used on either side, with a narrow shelf attached to the wall that is just large enough to hold a glass of water.

This bedroom is just 10 × 10 feet (3 × 3 meters). The platform of the bed includes drawers for clothing, and there's an open walk-in closet on the opposite wall.

The lamps next to the bed are modeled after those that once lit Parisian workshops, with a pendant that can be raised or lowered.

The coziness of this sweet little attic bedroom is enhanced with matching fabric for the headboard and wallpaper covering the walls and ceiling of the room. The bedding, curtains, rag rug, Victorian marble-top table and lamp, low table, and small, upholstered chair make this a perfectly feminine room.

UPSCALE DOWNSIZING

RIGHT:
Choose your artwork carefully. Roughan Interior Design designed this small New York City apartment, incorporating the owner's collection of art and handicrafts into the soft color palette.

OPPPOSITE:
A contemporary painting adds color to a sleek bedroom in a modern, urban apartment designed by Roughan Interior Design. A small desk in one corner provides an out-of-the-way workspace.

RIGHT:

A small bedroom accommodates the homeowners' teenage sons when they come home from college. Built-in bunks have deep drawers in the bases. Oversize pillow forms were covered with the intact pieces of an old quilt, each in a different pattern. Black-and-white photos and college pennants decorate painted wood lath walls. The room is compact, crisp, and well designed.

TIP: Patchwork quilts always add country charm and can be used as a wall hanging, a visual headboard on the wall behind a bed, and as a window treatment—a good end use for a worn quilt that can be cut apart and repurposed.

SHY ON CLOSET SPACE

Old houses often don't have enough closets for a modern family, especially since we seem to have accumulated more than our early forebears. Armoires were used in early American homes and still offer a good solution for bedrooms. In addition to providing a place to hang clothes, many are designed with concealed dresser drawers. While these items are large and take up space, they are practical, and you might not need much else besides the bed and night tables.

For a high-end look with a low-end cost, Ikea makes cabinetry, and a company called Semihandmade (semihandmadedoors.com) makes stylish custom doors for Ikea cabinets. In this way, you can create a wall of custom-look, built-in storage.

DRAPERY ADVICE

The way you decorate with draperies can help even the smallest bedroom feel spacious. Hang draperies as high as you can. Designers use this trick to make ceilings look higher: Place a drapery rod close to the ceiling, roughly two inches (5 cm) below crown molding or two inches below the ceiling. Extend the rod at least four inches (10 cm) beyond either side of the window so that the window appears wider and allows for optimum light.

Lined draperies block out light, and sheer curtains soften windows in a room that does not require a covering for privacy. Many designers prefer bare windows, and while I agree with their point of view, I do not like the way the black panes look at night. I usually suggest simple, sheer linen draperies hung with curtain rings from a rod. The drapes are light enough to pull across any window or expanse of glass at night. Simple curtains are a good choice for small rooms. Fussy draperies draw too much attention to the windows and often chop up the space, making the room look smaller.

LEFT:

Not enough closet space? A painted folk-art corner armoire works well as a closet. The oval Shaker box on top holds gloves and scarves. Some armoires have hooks on the insides of the doors for hanging belts, purses, and jewelry. Make every piece of furniture work for you.

OPPOSITE:

A built-in window seat provides a sleeping area for an occasional guest. By installing draperies, the homeowner can instantly provide privacy.

WINDOW TREATMENTS

Window treatments can baffle the most
experienced decorators. Start with the basics:
privacy, light control, and function. I am a minimalist
when it comes to bedrooms, and I like simple shades
or blinds. Shutters are nice for a clean look and
the ability to adjust light and air flow. All these
options are clean and unfussy. However, curtains
and draperies do absorb noise, create a warmer
atmosphere, and can provide opulence.

ABOVE:

Sheer curtains
allow light to
fill a room while
offering privacy. The
ottomans can create
different seating
arrangements.

RIGHT:

A writer loves the
view of the garden
from her bedroom
and had a desk
designed with
compact storage and
files along one wall.

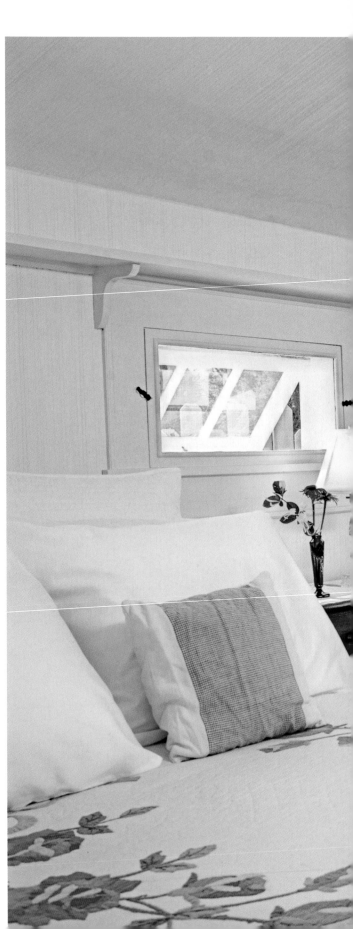

TIP: Place a desk next to a window to create a feeling of space when working. No window? A mirror visually expands the space; you will feel less cramped in a small area.

PILLOWS FOR ALL SITUATIONS

Pillows are an important part of making a bed look sumptuous. While I've heard many people complain about having to remove a pile of decorative pillows every night, most decorators and homeowners who would like the room to look as luxurious as possible love to buy pillows. If you know how to sew a straight line, they are also easy to make. Whether you are buying pillows or making them yourself, the following information might be useful.

Pillow Information

Decorative pillows usually come in even sizes. The most popular are 18 × 18 inches (46 × 46 cm) square for a standard-size sofa and 22 × 22 inches (56 × 56 cm) square for a deep sofa. A 20 × 20-inch (51 × 51-cm) size is appropriate for some sofas as well as on the bed. European pillows, often used as back pillows on a bed, are sometimes an uneven size, but most are 24 × 24 inches (61 × 61 cm) square or 26 × 26 inches (66 × 66 cm) square with a smaller decorative pillow, perhaps sixteen to eighteen inches (40–46 cm) square, placed in the front of a larger pillow. A deep sofa can handle two large pillows on each end, with a smaller pillow in the front, and two 18 × 18- or 20 × 20-inch (46 × 46- or 51 × 51-cm) pillows in the middle.

There are many styles and types of pillows. A bolster pillow adds a tailored look to a window seat, for example. Accent pillows emphasize or complement another part of the room, whether it's a color or pattern found in the curtains, wall paint, or floor covering. It might pick up one color found in a painting in the room.

TIP: As a rule, use five pillows on a queen-size bed and six on a king. If you want, put more on a guest bed since you don't have to make it every day. Plus, it will look fabulously welcoming to your guest.

OPPOSITE:

By using the same butterscotch yellow pattern on the walls, ceiling, and bed linens, this attic room exudes a cocoon-like quality. Plaid cushions on a wicker chair add contrast and texture. A wall lamp eliminates the need for a larger table to hold a lamp next to the bed. Without a need to cover the window, a simple valance adds a soft touch.

RIGHT:

Bedroom walls and ceiling are painted with Benjamin Moore's "Beacon Hill Damask," a rich shade of pale green. The bed is lush and inviting with pillows and layered coverlets.

BELOW:

Everything in this one-bedroom apartment was chosen for comfort, quality, and refinement.

CHECKLIST FOR A GUEST BEDROOM

I've always lived in a resort town, so having guests is inevitable. I've perfected the art of hosting, which includes making sure the room that I use for occasional visitors is pretty and comfortable. If you have a bedroom set aside for guests, it will take absolutely no time or effort to make it a welcoming retreat that they will appreciate.

1. Make the bed with high-quality sheets that are ironed, either by you or at a commercial laundry. They will look fresh and new even if they aren't.

2. Clean out at least one drawer for folded clothes and make room in the closet with good hangers.

3. Freshly cut flowers, along with a scented candle, on the dresser are nice extra touches.

4. Provide both soft and firm pillows and an extra blanket over the end of the bed. I am partial to a matelassé coverlet on top of the bed with a folded duvet across the bottom of the bed.

5. Fill a basket with a current copy of the local newspaper, a magazine of interest, and information about what's going on in town during your guest's stay.

6. Add a bottle of water and perhaps some fruit for a late-night snack to the basket.

7. Put a nightlight in the bedroom and bathroom.

8. A lightweight, one-size-fits-all bathrobe will be appreciated.

The draperies in this one-bedroom apartment elegantly extend from the ceiling
to the floor and cross the entire wall beyond the double set of windows.

6

CELEBRATING COLLECTIONS

Collecting starts out on an emotional level. Something speaks to you for unknown reasons. Perhaps it reminds you of something from your childhood. Often it doesn't have monetary value. For whatever reason, the experience of finding that one item leads to finding more. You want to relive the joy of discovery; but if you need to get rid of some of these items for space reasons, think of collecting as "temporary ownership." You enjoyed the collection. Now, move on.

However, if you can't part with the things you've amassed, you're in the majority. Recently, I was interviewing an interior decorator in a house she had just finished. It was sleek, modern, and devoid of a single extraneous item. It felt good. I wanted to live there—but only for about a minute. I missed a sense of humanity, and

maybe that's what "stuff" is all about. It represents who we are. These are the things that you have deemed important to make your new space feel personal. So, if you can't get rid of your collections, figure out a way to use them in your downsized home. If you're not going for a minimalist environment, find space for your collection: a tiny niche where you can custom-fit narrow shelves, a shelf above the sink, the top of the kitchen cabinets, under the cabinets, a dead corner, a hallway, or a glass-front cabinet. All you have to do is narrow your focus on that one problem. Don't look at the big picture. Look for new ways to display what you absolutely want to keep. You may be surprised to find creative solutions.

For example, a newlywed had a collection of blue willowware platters that were inherited from

A gardener collects watering cans. He has chosen the best and most useful to keep. The secondhand furniture was painted in cheerful enamel colors, and all the cans are artfully lined up on the bottom shelf of the sideboard.

her grandmother. Not only are they beautiful and useful, they also have great sentimental value. But when she moved into her new husband's tiny home, it was already crammed with the furniture he had inherited from his parents and grandparents. Fortunately, his attitude was "there's always room for more." This is a couple who reveres things from their families' pasts. With no window over the kitchen sink, they custom-fit a shelf between the kitchen cabinets on either side of the sink to display the blue willow, which is used for family get-togethers and holiday meals.

OPPOSITE:

A homeowner painted a table to showcase a collection of sea-related objects in an artful display. Notice that the combination of items was carefully arranged to look as though they were casually placed there, in keeping with the character of the collection.

BELOW:

A collection of blue willowware and cobalt glass vases is displayed on a narrow shelf over the sink in the kitchen. Crammed together, they make a statement. The glass vases are in constant use.

When inveterate antique "pickers" found a collection of industrial-size spools of thread at a flea market, they also used their creativity to find a way to display them in a small sitting area at one end of their kitchen. Sixteen spools of the same color were arranged in rows and framed in a Lucite® box for hanging. The entire collection makes up two horizontal rows filling a wall over the love seat. This is a fine example of how collections of any sort can be artistically arranged for visual interest. Other ways to create a display might be to arrange the spools on a narrow shelf around a room, or in a large basket. Look at what you have and see how many different ways you can dream up for display or use.

AN EDITED VERSION

A recently divorced best-selling author downsized to a house that could accommodate her esoteric collections from years of travel. While everything had once filled much larger rooms, she was determined to display everything on one wall in the living room of her smaller space. "I like things a bit worn, colorful, and with a back story," she says. "I admit, editing down wasn't easy, but I kept only things that didn't remind me of what my husband and I had bought together. I'm starting over with only my favorite things. I deliberately left space for more paintings that I intend to buy for my new life. But for now, I want to give each piece breathing room before adding another."

LEFT, ABOVE:
A collection of industrial spools of thread is displayed in Lucite boxes.

LEFT, BELOW:
A bay window provides an area for more collectibles, with a shelf above for paintings.

RIGHT:

A wall is filled with an edited collection amassed from years of travel. The sofas, pillows, rug, coffee table, and small folk-art piece were just part of the owner's furnishings from a larger home. Worn, colorful, and rustic, each piece adds comfort to the downsized space. Fresh flowers are essential to the homeowner's well-being.

OPPOSITE:

Narrow shelves in a retro kitchen hold a collection of turquoise bottles. A large painting is unexpected over the narrow counter space but is perfect for brightening the dark walls. The colors all work together.

LEFT:

With no outdoor space, an orchid collector replaced a window in a bedroom with a door to open onto a small, enclosed deck. His collection of orchids hangs on the fence. With newly created access to this area, he added an outdoor shower to the space.

TABLESCAPES

A tablescape is an artistic arrangement of items that complement each other within the small area of a tabletop. It is like creating a three-dimensional painting with objects. The items might be related in subject matter, like a collection of boxes or baskets. They might be similar in color, or they may be objects of different sizes, textures, and shapes. One of my favorite decorators was a master of tablescapes and loved using shades of brown in all his interior designs. He always advised: "Select objects of different heights, and mix materials like glass with wood so you have a combination of light and heavy, subtle and dark. If you arrange your collectibles artfully, you'll enjoy changing them from time to time as your interests evolve." Rather than creating clutter, you will have created an artistic presentation with the things you love. Let's face it. Americans love to shop. We are consumers.

Decluttering as a necessity for downsizing may not resonate well with everyone, so why not simply condense? Make collecting work for you by finding ways to edit selectively and exhibit in style. This is a work in progress. The accessories are as important as the furniture.

BELOW:
This arrangement combines glass items, which allow light to pass through, with dark objects in a variety of heights and shapes on a dark brown table. The fresh bouquet of white peonies in a glass vase enlivens the arrangement.

OPPOSITE:
Grouping framed family photographs on one table usually makes a stronger statement than when they are spread about. Many homeowners find comfort from family photos. Consider keeping them together in the bedroom.

TIP: The secret to using "clutter" for character is making sure it's all useful for you.

USE WHAT YOU HAVE

A woman with many treasured items bought a 1,000-square-foot (92.9-square-meter) cottage and was determined to fill it with her collectibles. She managed to fit them all in without making the house feel cluttered. She says, "The secret is making everything work for you." Here are a few of her tips.

→ Use a bench for seating on one side of a kitchen table. The bench takes up less space and can be tucked under the table when not in use.

→ In a small kitchen, make each area useful. For instance, designate a corner for making coffee. Use a shelving unit to hold a collection of coffee mugs and the space underneath for the coffeemaker.

→ To expand the eye, paint floors, walls, and ceiling white, linen, or gray. These colors make great backgrounds for displaying collectibles!

→ Feature a collection of mismatched, pretty vintage plates and glasses by hanging evenly spaced, narrow shelves on one wall. This displays the plates and glasses and keeps them easily accessible.

→ Track lighting illuminates an entire room and takes up very little space.

→ If you have a quilt that you can't part with, consider hanging it behind the bed, especially if your bedroom is small with no room for a real headboard. To keep the room from looking "recycled," cover the bed with beautiful lush bedding, a fluffy duvet, or a matelassé coverlet.

→ Lucite furniture, like a chair or side table, is marvelous for small spaces. Because it's transparent, it takes up less visual space, complements old pieces, and keeps small spaces from seeming cramped. I love it when paired with an antique desk or next to a traditional slipcovered sofa.

→ It might not seem practical, but placing a bed in front of the windows frees up wall space for a dresser or a storage cabinet for your collections.

→ If you're a collector and you lean toward vibrant colors and patterns, keep the rest of the room soft and calm. This doesn't mean that a small room should always be painted white. You can choose among thousands of colors to create an interesting, quiet background for any room.

→ Consider using a table as a desk and pairing it with a farmhouse chair. Create a niche for an office wherever possible and where you know you'll feel comfortable. It might be in a corner of the living room, a bedroom, or even in a hallway. An unused closet can easily be turned into an office space as well. Remove the doors, or use them to hide your work at the end of the day.

→ Make your rooms doubly useful: An office space might also work as a dining area. Design one end of a room as if it's completely separate, with a bench or love seat against the wall, a table in front of it, and a desk chair on the opposite side.

→ Bare windows open space. If you need a window covering for privacy, consider simple shades like bamboo, matchstick, or Roman fabric shades.

→ Cover a bathroom window with a curtain made from cheesecloth. This fabric creates just enough privacy while allowing light to filter through. It's a soft, feminine look, inexpensive, and totally unexpected.

COMFORT FROM MEMORIES

Not everyone wants a streamlined home. A world traveler and art collector finally downsized when he inherited his mother's saltbox-style house. The interconnecting rooms were small, and the house lacked architectural interest. But he treated each room as a miniature art gallery, making it a haven for his retirement years. Lacking a dining room, he created a dining area in a hallway where the ceiling sloped and filled the walls with his art collection. When not in use for serving a meal, he has an ever-changing group of pottery and interesting collectibles. The art in each room makes up for the lack of character in the architecture.

An antique table has a leaf for extension, but for everyday use, it is covered with collectibles that are put away when he entertains. The key to success here is being dedicated to removing things, which means having a place to put things away when space is needed, or repurposing them. For example, a large piece of pottery can hold a plant as a centerpiece. If you have interesting art and collectibles, make them the focal point of your home.

RIGHT:

A low wall in a dining alcove serves as a gallery for an art collection. When not in use, the table holds a display of three-dimensional objects.

A small, windowless
room was perfect for
a dining room. Since
the space has no view,
this homeowner used
the walls to create
visual interest with
her collection of
handicrafts around
the room.

PART II

INSPIRATIONAL LIVING

It takes discipline to get rid of the things you truly don't need or use but are emotionally attached to. However, the first step to downsizing is to rid yourself of things that simply won't fit into your smaller space, no matter how much you'd like to keep them. Don't get stymied by this. While it doesn't help to know that you're not alone, getting rid of things, especially things that have sentimental or emotional value, is hard for everyone. Everyone ultimately finds a system that works for him or her through trial and error. Those who have endured the process express the same sentiment: "Once you get into it, each item you let go of actually gives you a freedom of spirit. Letting go is a very cleansing feeling. It lightens you. It frees you to move forward rather than look back. It's like a diet: The more you lose, the better you feel." The following lifestyle stories are examples of how people in various stages of their lives have downsized with style. Their stories and pictures of their new spaces will be inspiring.

7

MOVING TO A NEW SPACE

FAMILY HOME REPURPOSED

In 1980, a couple bought a large family house in a small town, where they raised three daughters. After thirty-six years, they sold it and downsized to one half of a duplex house in the country. Since they sold their family home for more than the purchase price of the new house, they were able to renovate and make the new space over to suit their current needs. "I loved living in town," the homeowner says, "but now the girls have their own homes and their own children, and it was time for us to downsize." Not yet ready to retire, the couple says that after years of walking to work, they are surprised at how much they are enjoying the commute from town at the end of their workday. They note: "Sometimes we miss not being able to walk everywhere, but we like the peace and quiet. It's just different."

The new house is less than half the size of their original home. They say it is the perfect size for this chapter in their lives. With two small bedrooms and a bath upstairs and a bedroom and bath downstairs, there's room for their children to visit. They lived through the agony of renovation but say it was worth it, as the new space is perfect. "It has a more contemporary feeling," they say. "It's so much easier because the maintenance in an older home can't be minimized. Now everything is new and updated."

Like everyone in their situation, the biggest problem this couple had was getting rid of things. "It took almost a full year," she says. "First, I weeded out the 'no longer needed' items and donated them to the local thrift shop. That was the easy part.

OPPOSITE:
The living room flows into the dining area and kitchen, creating one large space. The furnishings are all white. Turquoise and green plants punctuate the space.

Then, we held several yard sales and gave our daughters whatever they wanted for their homes. Getting down to the last of our possessions was the hardest," she recalls. "Figuring out what we wanted to keep and what we wanted to buy new was another hurdle." In the end, they kept very little. Their advice is: "Give yourselves a reasonable deadline, if possible. Don't think you can do this job overnight."

Many people find that after living with possessions for several decades, they look forward to divesting and replacing older items with new furnishings that represent a new and often liberating lifestyle. They sometimes find, too late, that it wasn't a good idea to use what they already had when moving on. It's harder to get rid of things after you've moved than before. "Fewer possessions means less care," the homeowner says.

The new house is easy because they can live on one floor. With a small entryway, an open living room with a fireplace, a dining area, and a modern kitchen, plus a bedroom and bath downstairs, this house works for them. With two more bedrooms and a bath upstairs, they always have room for their daughters and their families to visit, and most of the time they can ignore the second floor. "Renovating can be expensive," she says, "but we're never moving again, so we wanted it to be just right."

When remodeling, the couple reconfigured the space for their current needs. In order to enlarge the kitchen, they divided what was once an additional first-floor bedroom into two parts and used the larger section to expand the kitchen. The smaller space became an office. By removing the kitchen wall facing the living room, they were able to install a kitchen island and stools for a casual meal. The removal of the wall also created a modern, open floor plan with three different uses. The first floor is now one open room where the living room, dining area, and kitchen flow into one another. French doors open from the dining area to a spacious outdoor deck that doubles their living space. The homeowner says it was important to

HOW DO YOU MAKE
A SMALLER HOME COMFORTABLE
WITHOUT LOSING A SENSE OF STYLE?
EMBRACE THE SIZE AND
MAKE IT AN ASSET.

OPPOSITE, TOP LEFT:
A collection of canes was acquired one at a time. Most were found at a local thrift shop. The painting is one of many that came with the move. "I couldn't get rid of the paintings so I brought them all, and they lean against walls for now," the homeowner says.

OPPOSITE, TOP RIGHT:
One of the two upstairs bedrooms has a trundle daybed for visiting family.

OPPOSITE, BELOW:
The dining area opens onto a deck, doubling the size of the home's living space. The deck provides an outdoor living and dining area all summer long.

make this living and dining area comfortable and maintenance-free. "Our main priority," she explains, "was to have a kitchen and dining-room table, both inside and out, that would accommodate our entire family—children and grandchildren." A long table fills one end of the deck, and a brown wicker wraparound sofa provides comfortable seating at the other end. "Now our lifestyle is much more relaxed, and we are more likely to eat at home than go out for a meal."

Each piece of furniture in the house was carefully chosen to make the most of the space. There are no knickknacks on the tables, and paintings lean against the mantel so they can be changed at will. The kitchen, like the rest of the house, is painted white and has marble countertops, painted wood cabinets, and a white subway tile backsplash. They used green plants to introduce a clean, fresh color scheme to go with the minimal approach to downsizing. "I chose top-of-the-line appliances and fixtures for the kitchen and bathrooms but saved where it wasn't necessary

BELOW:

The deck is furnished with a wraparound sofa, which is enhanced by gray and orange pillows. There's room for a long banquet table that seats all the kids and grandkids.

RIGHT:

A small kitchen was enlarged by taking away space from a second bedroom and removing a wall, opening the kitchen to the living area. A marble-top island provides casual seating. The outdoor deck is to the left.

in order to get the look without spending a lot," she says, pointing out the inexpensive deck furniture and an oversize outdoor umbrella from a discount retailer. All the outdoor fabrics are weather-resistant.

Without the burden of a large family home, this couple has more free time for traveling and family.

TIP: Don't be unrealistic about making room for the activities that are important to you. If you have to make a choice, sacrifice space that doesn't provide for as much pleasure.

CREATING A PLAN FOR STREAMLINING

THE FOLLOWING SUGGESTIONS APPLY TO DOWNSIZING, BUT CAN COME IN HANDY IF YOU SIMPLY WANT TO STREAMLINE AND DECLUTTER YOUR CURRENT HOME. LOOK AT DOWNSIZING AS A JOURNEY TO A CREATIVE, COMFORTABLE LIFESTYLE AND A NEW PATTERN OF LIVING.

BEGIN WITH a notebook. Go room by room and make a list under the heading "Things I Absolutely Cannot Live Without."

AFTER YOU'VE CHOSEN which items to part with, photograph each one that you feel sentimental attachment to. Also photograph the items you intend to keep, and put them in the notebook. If you're moving or rearranging your space, you can decide which item goes in which rooms later. What doesn't make the cut, goes.

ALLOW one hour to sift through one drawer or one coat closet, and remove as much as possible. Come back for a second look at another time.

REFINE AND REDUCE bookcase space.

GO THROUGH old magazines and rip out pages with info you want to keep. Make a small filing box for "recipes," "decorating," "personal," and other categories in which to store your clippings, or scan the pages and save them in a folder on your computer.

WEED OUT worn or duplicate items from kitchen drawers. Replace only the essential items. Small items, like whisks, funnels, veggie peelers, and mixing spoons, are useful everyday utensils. When was the last time you bought a new broom? Buy only one of everything you need, and buy the best.

IF YOU'RE MOVING into a smaller space, take inventory of the pieces of furniture you feel you "can't live without" and eliminate one item. Next, eliminate another item, continuing in this fashion until you've let go of everything that simply won't fit. Once it's gone, you won't miss it.

STARTING WITH a clean palette is much easier than working around what you bring to your new, smaller space.

COMPARE the size of the rooms in your new home with the size of your current rooms. If your new living room is the size of your old bedroom, be realistic about what furniture will fit where. A king-size bed may have to be exchanged for a queen in order to make the new bedroom feel more spacious. Plus, the fewer pieces you need, the more you can spend on top-of-the-line products.

REEVALUATE what changes you want to make to your lifestyle. For instance, think about how you want to entertain and what you like doing at home (read, cook, watch TV, craft, etc.).

DETERMINE your priorities: comfort, good design, space for family visits, less maintenance, a minimalist style, or room for memorabilia. They will enable you to design your downsized home for maximum enjoyment.

A DECORATOR'S HOME FOR ONE

After living in rented spaces for many years, a single interior designer bought a small house in Florida. "It was smaller than any place I had lived, but it was the best I could afford. It was a falling-down wreck. But I took my time and, little by little, created a jewel box," he says. "While it's only 850 square feet [79 square meters], I've pulled out all my decorating tricks to make it luxurious. The bonus was a tool shed that I converted into a second bedroom for occasional guests."

The tiny kitchen was the biggest challenge for this former private chef who loves to cook and entertain friends. However, with a good-size deck and mostly good weather year-round, he is able to entertain by creating meals ahead of time and serving them outdoors. "I built a long table from a plank of wood that easily seats twelve to fourteen," he describes. "The built-in bench spans the fence that defines the edge of the deck, and I have benches at each end of the table. This enables me to fit chairs on one side. I got them at a seconds shop. Aren't they great?" This homeowner is known for his clever and unique decorating style and knows how to add refinement to the tiniest rooms. "It's all in the details," he explains, "and good, comfortable furniture." He built a pergola over the seating area on the deck, then hung antique cobalt-blue glass lamps for unexpected elegance. This area now feels like a separate room. "I always use my best china, silverware, and oversize French linen napkins to make a table decadent," he says.

ABOVE:

Pierre Deux fabric on the inside of glass cabinet doors, a collection of ceramic plant holders, and paint provide bursts of color. The blue hanging lamps were found in an antique shop. The round window lets light into the bathroom on the wall's other side.

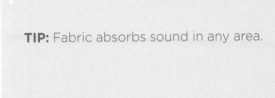

TIP: Fabric absorbs sound in any area.

"I found monogrammed linens at the flea market in L'Isle-sur-la-Sorgue in the south of France. It's not my monogram, but who cares? It's so easy to create luxury in a rustic setting like this deck."

The house started as a fixer-upper and was just one large open space. However, the owner was able to divide the room in half with a wall to create a bedroom and bath on one side and the living room/kitchen on the other. French doors at the back of the house open to an enclosed deck that is right off the kitchen and features a privacy wall of shells and a fountain that the owner built "one shell at a time." In this neighborhood, the lots are tiny and houses were built close to one another. The trickle of the fountain is a pleasant distraction from the ambient noise of the street and surrounding houses.

OPPOSITE:

The tool shed was converted into a luxurious guest bedroom. A French door lets in light, and a curtain at the end of the bed provides privacy. The graceful window was set into the front of the shed for more light and to keep the room from feeling closed in.

ABOVE:

Outdoor dining is romantic when the hanging lamps are lit, and the table is set with oversize linen napkins and ornate eighteenth-century silverware found at a flea market. The table was made from a plank of wood, and the legs were purchased from a lumberyard.

During his years as a private chef, this homeowner traveled with wealthy employers who had homes in different countries. Over the years, he acquired an appreciation for living well. His good taste and savvy shopping skills at flea markets in places like Paris and in trade shows and antique shops around the world have earned him a reputation in the interior-design business. His style can be described as a little bit funky with a whole lot of substance. "I look for great stuff at great prices everywhere I go and combine flea-market finds with unusual antiques." Everything he buys has to have an interesting quality. For example, he collects all sorts of unusual hinges and knobs—a feature that distinguishes the houses he decorates.

ABOVE:

Neutral colors are used throughout the living room with a variety of textures from seagrass chairs, velvet on the sofa, and sisal carpeting. The homeowner adds a bright bouquet of fresh flowers for a burst of color. A grouping of family photographs in a variety of interesting frames sits on top of the dresser and the trunk, which is used as a coffee table, holds extra blankets. The sofa was an estate-sale find.

OPPOSITE:

In the kitchen area, a window seat, small table, and bistro chair provide indoor eating space for two. Greenery outside creates privacy. Starfish line the window.

ABOVE:
Found silver trophy cups are used to hold silverware. "I use good silver every day," says the homeowner, "and I don't mind polishing. It's worth it."

OPPOSITE:
An old tool shed was turned into a sumptuous guest bedroom with built-in storage under the bed and in a bookcase. A stained-glass window lets in light and adds a wonderful detail along with the paneled walls. *Ladies at the Opera* is an elegant touch.

Although his house is small, his furnishings are not miniature. He says, "To make a statement, use a few large, good pieces rather than filling a room with lots of small furniture." Two large seagrass wingback chairs and a velvet love seat in the living room provide comfortable seating. But he points out a chest of drawers as his favorite piece: "It looks good and serves as a dresser since I don't have room for one in the bedroom, which is just on the other side of the wall."

Matchstick Roman shades are his signature window treatment. "I can't use up visual space with curtains or drapes," he says, "and their natural color works with the rest of the room." The living room is open to the yellow kitchen, which is at once functional, aesthetically interesting, and very compact. "I love collecting, so it's hard to limit my stuff," he says, "but I know what pots and pans I always need, so that part is easy. I store them under the sink. It's the things I've collected, like my ironstone, that need reining in."

An inveterate collector, this homeowner has definite ideas about displaying his possessions. A set of white ironstone bowls lines narrow floor-to-ceiling shelves on one wall, opposite the love seat in the living room. When a collection is all one color, it can be more dramatic and less jarring in small spaces than a jumble of patterns and colors. Another group of white ironstone pitchers sits on top of the kitchen cabinets for an eye-catching display. "I use these pitchers from time to time," he notes, "but mostly I like the way they look."

Yellow McCoy plant holders line a shelf along the back of the kitchen sink and are brought into service when needed. "They make a strong colorful statement that goes with the kitchen scheme," the owner says. With very little drawer space, he keeps

silverware on hand in found silver goblets. A large silver trophy cup holds wooden spoons, and large mixing bowls contain fruits and vegetables on the narrow countertops. "It's worth polishing silver to have these things," he adds. The glass cabinet doors are covered with curtains made from Pierre Deux fabric remnants found in Provence, France. They hide a myriad of dry goods. A curtain under the farmhouse sink, found in a salvage yard, hides pots and pans.

"I wanted the bed in the shed to be luxurious," the homeowner says. "My brother is a carpenter, and he built a platform with deep drawers under the mattress. He also built the wall-to-wall bookcase on one side of the room and narrow built-in shelves on the other to hold a variety of interesting collectibles." An oil painting called *Ladies at the Opera* hangs over the bed. "I think good art is an important accessory. No matter how small the space, it should feel and look expansive," he concludes. "Always do the unexpected."

WHEN THERE'S MORE THAN ONE

EVEN IF YOUR HOME IS SMALL, YOU CAN FIND CREATIVE WAYS TO ENTERTAIN ELEGANTLY, WHETHER IT'S DINNER FOR FOUR OR A HOLIDAY BUFFET PARTY. AND THERE'S ALWAYS A WAY TO FIND SPACE FOR AN OCCASIONAL OVERNIGHT GUEST.

1. If there isn't room at a table to seat more than one, create two small seating areas.

2. Casual meals can be served on a coffee table in a living room if there's no dining area.

3. Make a temporary table for buffet-style entertaining by placing a piece of plywood on top of two folding sawhorses from a lumberyard. The length of the plywood can be custom-cut to fit your space. Pad the top with cotton batting or use a quilt as a table cover. It's easy to set up and easy to put away.

4. Install a shelf on a piano hinge to create a temporary table to seat one to three people. When not in use, it can fold down flat.

5. If you have outdoor space in which to entertain, make it as elegant as your indoor space for entertaining.

6. You can be a bit selfish when you only have yourself to please. Buy what you love and display it proudly.

7. Choose furniture that provides more than one function. The top of an ottoman might provide additional seating, and the inside can be used to store extra linens.

8. Use space imaginatively rather than conventionally. For example, plastic storage boxes for extra bedding and linens can fit under the bed.

9. Open shelves can hold everyday essentials if they are contained in interesting ways.

10. No linen closet? Neatly fold extra towels and sheets for guests and tie them with a satin ribbon. Place them on open shelves wherever you can find space: in a hallway, above a toilet, or on a bedroom wall.

11. Consider a single daybed that doubles as a sofa to make room for an occasional overnight guest. There are many sleek products on the market. To create privacy when you have company, use a fold-up room divider.

KEEPING IT ALL AND MAKING IT WORK

Many times circumstances, like a career change, can dictate a move that requires downsizing because the cost of real estate is much higher in the new area. And often we don't have the luxury of waiting until the market goes down to buy at a better price.

When one couple bought a smaller home in a more expensive state than the one where they had lived for many years, the homeowner, who is a collector, recalls, "I had no intention of getting rid of anything." Making room for everything became a passion.

Many builders make up for a small footprint with high ceilings and lots of windows. Some homeowners opt for an all-white palette to achieve a feeling of space, but others like a colorful environment and can't live without their collections. This homeowner simply can't pass up a good yard sale, auction, or flea market and has been known to travel great distances in search of one more piece of yellow pottery. She never feels she has too much. "I like to be surrounded by the things I love. It gives me comfort when I look at them, and I remember every buying experience," she says.

"We chose a color scheme of yellow and white and added touches of blue to unify all the rooms," she notes. "Then it was just a matter of eliminating anything that didn't fit the color scheme. That was the first step." Gathering everything from sea glass and seashells to vintage fabrics and furnishings, she furnished their home entirely with her finds. Complementing her innate gift for finding and

arranging, her husband embraced the challenge to build just the right shelf to house a collection, retrofit a corner, or find a niche for a window seat. As an avid cook, he says the little galley kitchen was the greatest challenge. "But everything a good cook needs is in this little L-shaped space," he points out, including a washer and dryer as well as a built-in refrigerator in the back hall closet. "The trick is in the careful selection of just the right utensils and great organization," he explains. "Everything you buy should be top-of-the-line, so you don't need two of anything."

While there seem to be more collectibles than there is room for, this homeowner enjoys the constant satisfaction of moving things around until they look just right to her. "I'm the judge and jury, so more always looks better to me," she says. She loves finding more spaces for new shelves and simply rearranging when desired. She feels that out

ABOVE:

The only way to fit an antique wrought-iron bed in the downstairs bedroom was to position it across one corner. Bed linens from France, colorful paintings on the walls, and a warm color palette make the room inviting and reflect the design of the rest of the house.

of sight can mean out of mind, so she arranged her dishes artfully on narrow shelves or hung on walls, where they are always visible and ready to be used.

This house was a model home built in the 1980s in a planned community. It is smaller than many subsequent homes built in the area. Furnishing the house on a budget was a challenge, but these homeowners were certainly up to it and found that it fit with their passion for foraging. They chose the blue-and-yellow color scheme because it is cheerful, brightens the space, and complements the collectibles, like the grouping of plates and pottery they owned. Wherever there is the smallest, narrowest area, they have found an ingenious way to create a useful built-in feature, whether it is a lighted cabinet next to the fireplace or a built-in dining area where as many as ten people can squeeze together for a meal. "We don't often have that many, but when we get together with friends, we sometimes have to get very cozy," she says.

The house is one and a half stories high, with a layout that includes an entryway leading to the living room, where the ceiling is open to the rafters. There's a galley kitchen at one end of the living room, as well as a small dining area. French doors open onto a patio and yard surrounded by evergreens. The custom-built banquette has storage in the back of the benches to hold large trays. Small appliances are stored in the space under the hinged seats.

A small bedroom and bath occupy the front of the first floor, and upstairs there's a loft overlooking the living room. "We have the television set and a daybed up there, and lots of books," she points out. "They're all in the bookcase niche above the daybed." A small master bedroom and bathroom are also upstairs. A desk in one corner of the bedroom serves as an office.

Yellow walls throughout the house create sunshine, and windows in the gable ends of the living room bring in natural light. Patterns and textures from the slipcovers and framed botanical prints on the walls liven up the interior decoration. Bare floors are made of bleached pine. "I just touch up [the floorboards] here and there when they get scuffed," the husband says. "We like the

OPPOSITE:
There is clever storage everywhere. The built-in banquette seats lift up to provide space for trays and small appliances.

LEFT:
A cupboard houses a collection of blue-and-white willow plates and yellow McCoy pottery that emphasizes the overall blue-and-yellow color scheme.

distressed look." Not wanting a streamlined or minimal environment, this couple feels best when surrounded by oversize, comfortable furniture and lots of knickknacks. Three overstuffed sofas anchor the living room, creating a seating area around a painted yard-sale coffee table. Rather than consisting of lots of small pieces, this arrangement lends comfort to the room. However, the homeowner admits, "I can always make room for one more accessory."

These homeowners have advice for others who live in small spaces: "Look at every area, every corner, every niche for storage space. Look up and under, and you will be surprised at how you can manage to find clever ways to house what you own and avoid clutter. In a small house, it's a fine balancing act between collecting, storing, and displaying."

The homeowners like to entertain casually with their neighbors. They go from house to house, often starting the first course of a meal in one house and moving to others for each successive course. "All the houses have small kitchens," she notes, "so this is a great way to put a meal together for a group of friends."

TIP: A COLLECTION ALWAYS WORKS BEST WHEN IT IS USEFUL AS WELL AS VISUALLY INTERESTING.

Whether decorating their home or entertaining, these homeowners have found a casual approach that works with the size of their house and their particular lifestyle. "And that," they say, "makes everyone comfortable in our home."

OPPOSITE:
The living room is one
and a half stories high
and opens to the dining
area and kitchen, creating
an open, airy feeling that
belies its small space.
All the furnishings and
collectibles were lovingly
acquired at yard sales,
auctions, and flea markets.

LEFT:
Entertaining outside on
the patio extends the living
space in the summer. The
homeowners made the flags
for a birthday celebration.

129

ADVICE FOR EQUIPPING A SMALL KITCHEN

WHEN THESE TWO COOKS SET UP A TINY GALLEY KITCHEN FOR MAXIMUM EFFICIENCY, THEY HAD DEFINITE IDEAS ABOUT HOW TO DO IT. HERE ARE SOME OF THEIR SUGGESTIONS.

1. Good planning and organization is important when making meals so that you utilize the space in the most efficient way.

2. No matter how small your own kitchen is, it will seem large in comparison to other ones. For example, think about a galley kitchen on a boat where space is at a premium and every square inch counts. Besides, there is always a dead corner that can become a place for shelves.

3. Good lighting is important, especially over the work area. In a small kitchen, it's easy to flood the area with recessed lighting. The homeowner installed fluorescent bulbs specifically recommended for kitchens.

4. Play with fun and functional design elements. Because the neighboring houses are nearby, the owners hung two stained-glass windowpanes (found on one of their foraging trips) over each window for privacy and visual interest. Best of all, they don't block out the light.

5. Buy modular storage containers and organize everything for easy and practical use. A small kitchen takes a concerted effort to plan and arrange, but once it's designed for efficiency, making everyday meals or cooking for a group of friends will be a pleasure.

6. Organize small utensils like wooden spoons and spatulas in containers like a pottery crock, and hang baskets to hold fresh fruit and vegetables for easy access.

7. Hang a narrow shelf above the sink with a rack for wine glasses beneath it, much like those used in bars. The shelf can hold odds and ends that aren't used all the time, and the glasses don't take up precious cabinet space and still remain conveniently within reach. Once rinsed, they can be hung back on the rack to dry.

8. Maximize storage with cabinets. While some people might prefer open shelves, these homeowners put in as many cabinets as could possibly fit in the space. With cabinets, you don't have to be quite as neat.

9. Consider a butcher-block countertop for food-prep work. The homeowners replaced the existing countertop with a butcher-block one and extended it slightly to gain a few more inches of space.

10. Always buy the best tools and make sure you have the right size pans and skillets so that you only need one of everything. If you don't use it, lose it.

OPPOSITE:
The kitchen is compact and perfectly suited for a homeowner who is passionate about cooking.

8

DOWNSIZING TOGETHER

COMBINING HIS AND HERS

After knowing each other for several years, a working couple recently married and bought a one-bedroom apartment on the second floor of a two-story house. Having each lived in separate homes, the challenge was to combine their possessions into one small space so it would function well and showcase their individual tastes. "We are collectors. We love to travel. We have a passion and interest in wines from different regions," they said.

The stairway from the downstairs entry opens into a living room of average size that feels airy due in part to the glass doors that open to a deck with a view. This room flows into a dining area and an open, streamlined, sophisticated kitchen that functions better than its size would indicate. At the opposite end of the apartment is a compact master bedroom and luxurious bath.

Every room is filled with a commingled, eclectic mix of vintage and modern items. The only criteria that the couple use when buying something together are: good design, good value for the money, and that they love it and can't live without it. "This is a work in progress," she observes. "It's evolving, the way a good wine ages.

OPPOSITE:

A great example of mixing old and new is the juxtaposition of the chandelier, a prized vintage find, with a modern glass dining table. Each set of handmade plates is a different brown pattern. The chairs came with the apartment.

We travel every chance we get, each time returning with something we couldn't resist." For now, the apartment feels comfortably appointed, but they admit that as their travels expand over time, some things may have to go to make room for others.

Because of a demanding schedule (they both own retail stores), this couple wanted a maintenance-free apartment furnished in a way that would reflect their interests—a place that was aesthetically beautiful and comfortable—and where they most wanted to be at the end of the day. "I've always appreciated things that have stood the test of time, and I love combining them with new and well-designed objects of substance," she says. Everything they chose, from the wall coverings to the kitchen cabinets, was done with deliberate care. These apartment owners believe in buying locally, and, aside from the collectibles from their travels,

LEFT:
Accessories in the master bath were chosen for their soft seafoam color, echoing the countertop and tub surround. The antique mirror counterbalances the modern bathroom.

The partial wall in the bedroom creates storage space on one side, while leaving enough room for furniture in the bedroom. The soft relaxing paint color is "Interlude" by Benjamin Moore. Two Chinese Foo dogs and velvet pillows on a Pottery Barn sleigh bed give the room a punch of color. (Another fun detail: the retro phone.) One of the two Maine Coon cats, Margaux (a redhead named for red wine), enjoys her starring role. There's also a white cat, Meursault, named for white wine.

most of the furnishings in the apartment are from their fellow shop owners, artists, and craftspeople. They are simply passionate in the way they live, work, and involve themselves in their community.

In a time when people are building larger and larger homes and when decorating is done instantly, this couple has deliberately furnished a home that is personal and tasteful, is in scale with the size of the rooms, and reflects the places they've been.

"I love that everything in our home tells a story or reminds us of an experience," she says. "It's how I buy—with a passion. I have to love everything in my home, the clothes I wear, how we shop for food, and how we entertain our friends and family." Clearly, they are creating memories one item at a time.

This is a home that is accumulating layers of beautiful furnishings, accessories, and artwork that is evolving into personal expression. They are able to marry unlikely objects, such as antiques and flea-market finds, with current trends, and understand scale and proportion to the max. There is also restraint. Together, they have artfully

TIP: Lamplight in a room provides a warm and welcoming presence. A soft light left on in a front hallway, for those not yet home, is such a loving gesture. It exudes a feeling of coziness.

OPPOSITE, ABOVE:

An antique dresser holds an array of pink Depression glass, vintage seltzer bottles, and a 1950s Welch's wine bottle under the stairway. The marble lamp belonged to a friend's grandmother.

OPPOSITE, BELOW:

The open floor plan includes a living room with fireplace, a dining area, and a kitchen. White-painted floors and a muted palette of neutrals and browns are enlivened with accents of magenta from a pair of signed ballet slippers on a shelf, velvet pillows, a bouquet of roses in a vintage McCoy vase, and a woven throw. The champagne-cork side table reflects the couple's interest in wine. The wrought-iron and stone demilune table was found in a catalog, and the boots next to the fireplace are from the Paris Flea Market.

and with pride arranged their furnishings so that everything not only looks right but also feels right. Things are allowed breathing room. She admits, "I didn't decorate this apartment by myself," and advises, "Tap into talents around you wherever you can. I've got lots of friends with excellent taste, and I never hesitate to ask for help. A decorator friend gave me a lot of good advice, but I also relied on the influences of my mother and my grandmother, [and] even a neighbor from my childhood who had these wonderful '70s modern chairs that I coveted and now own."

Her partner adds, "Traveling is extremely stimulating. We've brought back lots of things, but

BELOW:

At the end of the day, the couple loves to come home to the view from their deck and enjoy a glass of wine. Vintage deck chairs, punctuations of orange pillows, and wooden wine boxes used as tables reflect the couple's interest in wine.

we shop carefully so we don't just amass items that we then have to find a place to display." With a shared interest in wine, their travels often take them to wine-producing areas, like France, Italy, and Spain, or closer to home, like Napa Valley, California. Trips to more exotic places like Peru, Morocco, Greece, and Turkey have yielded inspiration for different reasons.

Their decorating style seems to be the unexpected—something whimsical, campy, or obviously handcrafted is right at home with an inexpensive coffee table that, in this environment, is elevated in status and works perfectly. She says, "There's a perception that things have to be expensive to be worthwhile, but, as with wine, you can identify potential. Quality often comes with aging." Their home reflects how old things can be updated with newer accessories, such as an antique African map that adds genuine character to their luxuriously modern bedroom. "Bringing home that map is an experience we'll never forget," she says. And that pretty much sums up the joy of it all.

RIGHT:

The wallpaper in the living room is from Harlequin in a pattern called "Willow," and the Matisse etchings came from an antique show. The couple's most prized piece, the unglazed porcelain vest, was found in a Hong Kong gallery and made by artist Fiona Wong. They were so moved by her work that they hand-carried it home and were surprised that it survived. The wife won out over her husband with the horse-shaped clock and lamp. The final punctuation mark is a delicate "claret" bouquet of roses.

FOLLOWING PAGE:

The silver-mirrored subway tiles infuse glam. "I was skeptical," the homeowner says, "but once installed, I loved the look."

TIP: A mirrored backsplash in a small kitchen will work visual wonders.

PUTTING IT TOGETHER

WHEN IT COMES TO COMBINING OLD AND NEW, FOUND AND INHERITED,
THESE HOME OWNERS HAVE SOME TIPS THAT ANYONE CAN FOLLOW.

DOWNSIZING SHOULD BE DONE QUICKLY AND EFFICIENTLY

and without emotion if possible. Each of you will have things you are emotionally attached to,
but if it doesn't work in the new scheme, try to let it go or pack it away. The new space
doesn't have to be furnished or decorated all at once. A home that evolves
over time is usually the most satisfying.

THINGS DON'T HAVE TO BE EXPENSIVE

to be worthwhile, but they should be well-designed or have sentimental value. For example,
a beautiful shell is the perfect small accessory to add to an arrangement of items on a table.
Its color, shape, texture, and connection to nature make it worthy of display.

WHEN JOINING HOUSEHOLDS, SOME THINGS JUST HAVE TO GO,

but this gives you a chance to start over together
and buy what you love and what has meaning to both of you.

DECORATING IS AN OPPORTUNITY.

Make the most of the experience.

THERE ARE NO RULES

when it comes to decorating, but everything you put in your space should be comfortable, have a purpose,
and be aesthetically pleasing to look at. Otherwise, you have to ask yourself why you still have it.

DON'T BE AFRAID TO ASK FOR HELP.

Encourage your friends, or at least those you trust or whose taste you admire,
to offer suggestions and advice.

GET INSPIRATION EVERYWHERE YOU GO.

One of the homeowner's favorite places in London is Sir John Soane's Museum, where she was
transformed by the collection of antiquities and Hogarth engravings. "One of my favorite landmarks
in our town inspired me to be myself and trust what I liked," she explains. "There is inspiration
everywhere, no matter where you live. You don't have to go far to find it."

USE THE COLORS YOU LOVE

and that make you feel good. With a nod to their love of wine, this couple introduced accents
of magenta and claret into their neutral-and-brown color scheme.

BUY THE BEST YOU CAN AFFORD.

Quality over quantity is a good rule of thumb.

MERGING HOUSEHOLDS

After two middle-aged partners lost their spouses, they found love the second time around with each other. They each had homes they had lived in for a long time. Neither wanted to move in with the other, so they decided to sell both homes and look for one they could share. The problem was that each had amassed a houseful of furnishings, and one, now retired, had been an antique dealer in American folk art for over thirty years.

After selling both of their old houses, they bought a small Victorian gem to start a new life together, with one of the partners bringing two dogs into the mix. "We were faced with getting rid of a lot of baggage," one of the partners recounts. "It took a year to whittle down to the things we absolutely couldn't live without. I've been collecting antiques, interesting folk art, and art books for a lot of years, so we just had to find a way to make it work. A Victorian house seemed appropriate to showcase our collections. These houses are known for their ornate interior design."

Victorian-style houses are a great choice for people who are most comfortable surrounded by the furnishings and collections they love. These houses have history and embody the idea that a home can absorb a lot of furnishings and collectibles without seeming out of place.

However, Victorian houses, like other early American homes, are notoriously lacking in storage space. People during that era simply didn't have as many possessions to store away, so the couple needed to find new ways to create room wherever possible. The house had a small downstairs bedroom that they turned into a sitting room/library by designing a wall-to-wall, built-in bookcase on a wide, windowless wall. "Having all the art books in one place took care of one problem," one homeowner says. "Then we selected all the artwork that could possibly fill the walls [and hung them] in that room. Much of it relates to the art-book collection," he continues.

"We furnished this room with a sofa and two chairs brought from one of our former homes. It fit perfectly, and we really enjoy sitting in this room surrounded by artwork and books. It's very comfortable and comforting to have been able to fill it without buying anything new." Some people find that downsizing with things they've cherished is important when starting over.

A bay window in the dining room is typical of Victorian homes. It turned out to be the perfect spot for a built-in window seat, under which they created more space for books. Small shelves between the windows allowed for handicraft displays. Lighting was planned to highlight chosen pieces. Much of their early-American folk art and handcrafted furniture fit perfectly into this room.

BELOW:

The owners enjoy creating an elegant setting for dinner on the folk-art table, which is flanked with chairs by renowned craftsman George Nakashima. The bouquet of garden roses provides a lovely Victorian touch.

"Whatever we can use, we do," the homeowners say, "even if, at first, things don't seem to go together. But we like the central theme of honoring outstanding craftsmanship from any era."

Most Victorian-style houses were built between 1837 and 1910. Sometimes referred to as "painted ladies," they are quite decorative and include gingerbread trim. Some say they look like dollhouses, but Victorian architecture actually refers to styles that emerged in the period between 1830 and 1910 during the reign of Queen Victoria. Victorian style appealed to the romantic idea that homes, as well as clothing (think hoop skirts and yards of fabric), should be beautiful rather than just practical. Architects often borrowed details from French, Italian, Tudor, or even Egyptian styles to create different Victorian homes. For this reason, few Victorian houses look alike. This couple was attracted to this style of house because they felt it was a good background for their collections of folk art.

This house has a lovely stained-glass window at the top of the stairway that lets light filter into an otherwise dark area. The stairway wall provides a good expanse for more artwork. In the entryway below, the wall supports a narrow shelf to hold a collection of handmade baskets with one large painting above it. Most Victorian homes were

crammed with as many pieces of furniture, fabric, and accessories as possible. In that regard, this couple has followed tradition, furnishing their home with a decidedly personal approach. Each room is tastefully accessorized with whirligigs, old toys, weather vanes, early advertising posters, pottery, sculptures, and memorabilia on shelves and furniture. Renowned artist George Nakashima handcrafted the chairs (as well as the piano bench in the living room) that surround a painted folk-art table in the dining room. They are part of the owners' unique collection of handicrafts, family heirlooms, and furniture that make up their eclectic style and add to the character of the house.

Their approach, which was typical of the era in which the house was built, is an attempt to showcase both cultural interests as well as the belief that bareness in a room was a sure sign of poor taste. Another aspect of Victorian interior

RIGHT:

The living-room sofa fits neatly into the bay-window alcove. Two side chairs finish a comfortable seating area. While the grand piano fills the room, the joy of music overrules the need for more space. The floorboards are original to the house.

OPPOSITE:

A typical Victorian banister and newel post is seen in this house. The stained-glass window at the top of the landing is another feature of most Victorian houses and provides light for the wall of paintings.

TIP: If you want to store things that you can't part with and that don't fit into your space, know that you will need to rent storage space or find a home with a basement or attic.

TIP: Many gallery owners suggest that when hanging pictures on a wall, you "treat them as one item and create a layout on the floor before hanging." Spacing is crucial and requires adjustments before getting it just right.

design was the use of warm and subdued colors—gray or creamy backgrounds, deep rich walnut and mahogany with aubergine, wine, musty yellow, burgundy, and dusty hues. Typically, Victorian homes displayed busy patterned wallpaper and fabrics. A modern approach was used here, with ivory-colored fabric on upholstered furniture (acquired through an estate sale) and white walls. One of the owners had patterned upholstered furniture, but the other owner had a nice collection of rugs, so they decided to keep the rugs and replace the furniture. Downsizing often involves compromises like this.

Original floorboards are intact and in perfect condition. Persian area rugs lend a richness of texture and color in the rooms and hallways.

The owners are quick to point out the interesting floor pattern. Wide pine floorboards were used in the center of the dining room, where a carpet typically would have been placed. However, fir boards were laid in a pattern around the perimeter of the room, with mitered corners, much like the border of a quilt. This section was made from better and harder wood, as it was the only exposed area of the floor and received much wear and tear. These preserved floorboards are also found in the exposed areas of the living room. All these details are just as they were when the house was built, except for new coats of paint on the molding trim. "All this character was more important to us than large modern rooms," they say, "even though we still have boxes of things we couldn't part with and have no room for. But this house suits our aesthetic style. We feel comfortable surrounded by beautiful things, and this house, with its small, interconnecting rooms, is good for the way we live now."

RIGHT:

A collection of baskets is displayed in the entryway. The wall is perfect for paintings. The hallway and stairway were treated as one room.

OPPOSITE:

These colorful houses, located in San Francisco, are examples of "painted ladies"—Victorian-style homes whose exteriors are painted in three or more colors.

KEY ELEMENTS TO VICTORIAN-STYLE HOUSES

VICTORIAN HOMES HAVE MANY FEATURES THAT MAKE THEM A POPULAR CHOICE WITH HOMEOWNERS.

1. Most Victorian houses were built before 1910.

2. The exteriors are often decorated with elaborate wood and metal trim, commonly called "gingerbread." The siding on many Victorians is dressed up with scalloped shingles and patterned masonry.

3. The kitchen was always in the back of the house, while the garden was in the front.

4. Thanks to the arrival of plate glass in 1832, many Victorian houses have four-paned vertical sliding-sash windows.

5. These houses often have steep rooflines and many gables. Some have what is called a Mansard roof, which is flat-topped with windows in the side to maximize the space inside.

6. Victorian-style homes almost always have a wraparound porch. Ornamental spindles and brackets are another feature of the Victorian style.

7. These houses are often large and imposing and have complicated shapes with bays and wings in different directions. There are usually two or three stories.

8. Victorian houses had smaller rooms and less closet space than most modern homes, making each room feel intimate. Each room was often used for a specific activity.

9. Before the Victorian era, houses were painted one color: either beige or white. However, by the time this style of house was built, bright earth tones of sienna and yellow were in vogue.

9

REBUILD, RENOVATE, REPURPOSE

A BEACHSIDE COTTAGE

The smallest project that internationally known interior designer Kathleen Hay ever designed is just under 1,200 square feet (111 square meters). Her clients, a couple with three children, owned a small property in a seaside community. They wanted to build an elegant, maintenance-free cottage that would be sleek and modern for their vacation lifestyle. The completed beachside cottage is the perfect example of creative upscale downsizing with outstanding details, storage solutions, and architectural interest that are awe-inspiring.

Small by today's standards, the size of the lot was the most important factor when designing the house. The challenge was to create a comfortable home within this limited space. The owners would ultimately create an open floor plan with an average-size kitchen, dining area, living area, and mudroom, with a bathroom downstairs and three small, efficiently positioned bedrooms upstairs. They knew that the size of their new house would require built-in furniture with maximum functionality. The finished home is a wonderful example of space efficiency. They did not bring one thing to this house from their other home.

OPPOSITE:

Each of the three bedrooms has a full bath. All the beds were built in to maximize floor space. Floating bedside tables are equally space-saving.

Surprisingly, the house has three full bathrooms with elegant and comfortable showers and appropriate storage for towels and bath accessories. To meet the size and scale of the house, the furniture had to be custom-built. The campaign beds—a king for the master bedroom, a queen for another room, and twin bunk beds in the third—allow for storage drawers underneath so that there is no need for dressers. "You also avoid having bed skirts that can be a nuisance," Kathleen points out. And here's a clever feature: there's a center drawer at the end of the king bed for storing suitcases. Bedside tables float from the walls to avoid having legs that would make it more difficult to open the drawers under the beds. Swing-arm or hanging lamps provide bedside lighting. All the fixtures were chosen to fit a nautical theme. The couple used beadboard for the walls throughout the house. This gives each room a boat-like feeling, which suits the coastal location of the house.

The limitations of the square footage of the lot and the needs of the family for comfortable living required a talented architectural team, a reliable and skilled contractor/builder, and an interior designer who could think spatially. The limitations also required a creative plan for all the details

BELOW:
Sleek and modern, the living room is the hub of this small beachside cottage. Beadboard ceilings with recessed lighting and shutters on the windows create a streamlined silhouette. The armchairs swivel for conversation and television-watching.

OPPOSITE, ABOVE:
A lounge chair in the master bedroom creates a quiet corner for reading. Furniture in each bedroom is kept to the basics. The king-size bed and floating bedside table were custom-made.

RIGHT:

The neutral palette
has a calming
influence on the small
living area, which
easily seats six.

RIGHT:

The open floor plan accommodates a dining table that can seat eight to ten. The "floating" staircase is almost sculptural and makes the small space feel less confined. The front door opens into an elegant foyer.

that would showcase interesting, exciting ideas for the interior design. It was equally important to use materials that would prove, over time, to be practical and well-designed, to find ways to solve storage problems, and to take into consideration subtle things like traffic flow and how the family would be using the house. It was a challenge to fit all the required elements into the tight footprint.

A side door leads into a mudroom, although "mudroom" is too humble a word for this area. It is an "unwinding" space—a place to drop one's outer gear, sit on a cushioned bench to remove running shoes or flip-flops, and hang slickers and hats on pegs lining the wall. It's a room that receives the messiness of everyday living.

The downstairs bathroom might have been the usual powder room for guests, but instead of a window in this room, there's an exterior glass door that opens into an outdoor shower. What a luxurious idea it is to come home from the beach, step into the outdoor shower, leaving all the sand behind, and then right into the bathroom, without having to go back outside again. And voilà! A full bath has been created where there wasn't enough room inside for the shower.

Then there's the floating stairway with cable wires for handrails, making this utilitarian feature almost sculptural without taking up visual space the way a solid wall usually would.

The homeowners wanted a sophisticated year-round house, not too casual or beachy but clean and functional. They chose the furniture accordingly. Kathleen notes, "The neutral palette keeps 'visual noise' to a minimum, and a mix of materials and periods is the key to this [living] room's success." When you build small, you can spend more money on top-of the-line materials, opting for quality over quantity. Walnut, zebrawood, polished metal, marble, soft chenille, and pickled white oak floors combine beautifully and subtly into a varied layering of textures. The overall effect is a chic level of "kick-back" comfort and function appropriate for the beachside location.

The kitchen island, made of high-gloss walnut, seats five and is a casual place to serve an informal meal. The easy transition from the entryway to the kitchen, dining area, and living room makes the house feel luxurious. The simple, clean furnishings are low-maintenance to ensure easy, everyday living for the homeowners, as well as for when their grown children visit or when they have guests for the weekend.

LEFT:

The kitchen is a study in efficiency. The island houses trash and recycling bins and small appliances. Though the space is small, there was no compromise on the full-size, top-of-the-line appliances.

FOLLOWING PAGE:

A compact mudroom provides a place to take off shoes and hang hats and raincoats.

UPSCALE DOWNSIZING

IT'S ALL ABOUT THE DETAILS

ELEGANT TOUCHES ARE A MUST IN SMALL SPACES.
THEY HELP YOU FEEL THE LUXURY, NOT THE SMALLNESS.

1 Chrome hotel racks are used above the toilets for towels. They hold a lot, look good, and save space. No linen closet is required.

2 Frosted glass on the bathroom doors provides privacy but also allows light into tiny spaces.

3 There are lots of brilliant "look good, feel good" details that you can add to a bathroom, such as white penny-round porcelain tile on the floors or linear drains in the showers. For linear drains, a slightly slanted floor can allow water to drain at the back of the shower.

4 Built-in niches in walls for bath accessories offer efficient storage space and look great.

5 Peg hooks are a practical solution wherever you need to hang something. Wooden pegs along the mudroom wall and hooks on backs of bathroom doors help kids be neat and keep clothes and wet towels off the floor.

6 Pocket doors on tracks also save space, especially where a normal-size hinged door won't fit.

7 A coffee table with a shelf allows the tabletop to look clean and beautiful while still offering a place for newspapers or books.

8 You can use materials that are not typically found in specific rooms to create striking details. One example of this is the walnut trim that runs along the base of the kitchen cabinets. Beadboard is a good material for a beach house, but it should be applied seamlessly to keep it visually simple and elegant rather than distracting.

9 Seamless marble countertops and a continuous backsplash enhance the sleekness of the kitchen and make it appear larger.

10 A single large chandelier over the kitchen island lends a sense of weight and importance, so serving a meal in the kitchen feels less informal.

ABOVE:

Walnut is a high-end, unusual wood to use for the trim along the base of the kitchen cabinets.

RENOVATING AN OLD HOUSE

A couple bought a small cottage built in the 1800s on Nantucket Island, Massachusetts. They wanted to renovate the cottage, repurposing as much of the original material as possible in the restoration. Furthermore, they wanted the house to be designed with modern conveniences in a practical way without losing any of its original character. This was the challenge the owners of the property put forth when they approached the Massachusetts firm of Angus MacLeod Designs. The architects and designers at MacLeod helped creatively repurpose space and recycled materials. They modernized without losing a sense of the cottage's original design and addressed basic living issues in a practical yet visually exciting way.

The house was originally built by unskilled workers but was nonetheless charming because of its size and the proportion of the rooms. This was often the case with homes built in the early 1800s. If you are planning to undertake a similar renovation project, be sure to research and hire an experienced team of designers and craftsmen who understand the value of old houses and the importance of doing a responsible job. For those of you who might be considering an old home, consider consulting a professional restorer before committing to this kind of purchase.

One of the firm's signature interior features worth noting is graceful, curved doorways. Another is the ingenious sleeping loft space that they've designed into many of their projects. The architect says, "Arches and vaulted ceilings add femininity to a space, especially when there is a lot of wood involved; the yin to the wood's yang." The living room also functions as a guest room. A library ladder affords access to the loft above the big built-in window seat.

The designers spent a lot of time in salvage yards, where they found all the passage doors, French doors, knobs, interior windows, newel posts, and balusters. "It's quite laborious, picking through salvage. You never know what you'll find on any given day," they said. But everything in the house is of a piece; and while the upholstered furniture is new, its design is a nod to the past.

During the renovation, they also uncovered beautiful materials such as sheetrock walls and plywood floors behind the dropped ceilings, and they were able to repurpose all the wood.

BELOW:

A sleeping loft is accessed from a library ladder.

This is an ingenious way to create sleeping space.

OPPOSITE:

Layers of wall
coverings were
peeled back to reveal
the blue boards of
the original open-
stud structure. The
original milk paint
was peeling but intact
enough to dictate the
flavor of the entire
house going forward.
Insulation was added
on the outside to
showcase the room's
historic interior.

LEFT:

The second bedroom
was originally a
laundry shed. It is big
enough to hold two
ship's berths. Adding
a step down between
the beds created
headroom of 6 feet
4 inches (1.9 meters)
at the lowest point in
the room. The ceiling
was created from
the original flooring
on the second floor.
Each bed has storage
underneath.

OPPOSITE:

The attic was turned into a master bedroom suite. The French doors are salvaged. The gentle arch and wavy glass add character to the room, while the dropped ceiling was opened to expose the original rafters.

ABOVE:

The powder room can be accessed from the hall or bunk bedroom and also opens into an outdoor shower.

RENOVATING AN OLD HOUSE

WHEN YOU START A RENOVATION PROJECT, LISTEN TO THE PROFESSIONALS AND USE THIS ADVICE TO MAKE SURE EVERYTHING IS FEASIBLE FROM COST AND DESIGN PERSPECTIVES.

1 The key to a successful project is to love the house that you are planning to renovate. Renovating a historic house takes time and can be difficult. But it can be worth the effort, because you'll have preserved a link to the past. You are part of the history of the house.

2 Do your homework. Be sure you understand the difference between restoring a home to the original configuration, rather than to a modern version, of its architecture. Research houses in the area and from the period. Find a builder (and architect if necessary) who shares your passion for historical renovations.

3 As with any renovation, prepare a detailed budget and review it with your builder before you begin. Plan on adding twenty percent to most cost projections.

4 Keep your lifestyle and how you will use the house in mind before meeting with your builder or architect.

5 In the design phase, identify as many details as possible, such as fixtures, hardware, windows, and door trim. Consider the materials that were originally used to build the house. The design of the space should follow.

6 When landscaping, try to use indigenous materials and be realistic about what plants and bushes will do well in your area.

7 Be patient. If you're in a hurry to move in, you'll be tempted to cut corners that you'll regret once you're living in the house.

DIY COUNTRY STYLE

Many DIY decorating projects offer an opportunity to have the things you love and want in your home but can't afford right away. DIY does not necessarily mean compromise. Here's how one couple furnished their first home.

Deciding it was better to own than continue to throw money away on rent, a young couple left a large city apartment and moved into a three-room cottage in a seaside town. While they enjoyed the spaciousness of the apartment, they no longer wanted to live in the city and opted for downsizing inside space for more outdoor living. Built with Timberpeg® posts and beams, the cottage is one room wide with only three rooms in "railroad flat" configuration, one in back of the other: a living room, bedroom, and kitchen/sitting room combination with spectacular views from every window. There's a compact bathroom off the narrow hallway. The land on which the cottage is situated limits its size and any possibility for expansion. While it is a simple cottage, the homeowners nonetheless wanted it to reflect their love of country-style decorating and furnished it on a very strict budget.

BELOW:

A sitting area that is part of the kitchen is filled with yard-sale finds and DIY projects. Some paint, some fabric, and a glue gun are all it takes.

OPPOSITE:

The living room in a timber-peg, three-room house is furnished with yard-sale makeovers. The dark walls were brightened with a whitewash stain. The corner is filled with plants in a variety of containers on small tables of varying heights.

To keep the furnishings informal and carefree for beachside living, the homeowners scoured yard sales, auctions, and online bargain sites for their furniture. It would not take much to fill each room with basic, comfortable items. With a knack for DIY projects, they employed their own clever handiwork as well. In this way, nothing in the house would feel out of place with their casual design. They filled the room with items associated with country style, like rag rugs, cotton quilts, wicker baskets, and chintz. They wanted to offset the heavy timber beams and wood with a perky color scheme and lively fabrics.

For the living room, they chose green and white with accents of yellow to echo the grasses and flowers seen from the windows in that room. Blue and white with splashes of yellow were chosen for the sitting room and kitchen/eating area, while pastel colors were picked for the bedroom. The first thing they found at an auction was a wonderful bamboo sofa and chair (à la Ralph Lauren) that just needed new fabric. A polished chintz fern print was perfect. They wrapped and stapled the fabric to the wood on the underside of the cushions. A drop-leaf table from a yard sale was transformed with a refinishing kit and a stencil design. Unfinished furniture is perfect for people

who enjoy crafting. It is usually well made and provides a good background for wood stain, paint, and faux finishing techniques. The couple stained an unfinished wooden bench for no-fuss, no-muss seating. A wicker rocker found at a yard sale just needed a few throw pillows, which were a cinch to make with remnants of fabric sewn over pillow forms (from any craft or sewing shop). This chair is easily moved around when they want to sit on the deck off the kitchen.

A country hutch fits nicely into the corner of the kitchen and holds collectibles or chinaware. They spray-painted all sorts of paint buckets and containers for plants. No window treatments were necessary or desired in the living room; the key thing was to keep the views unobstructed with everything simple and streamlined and most of all, easy to maintain. For occasional privacy, they just drape one sheer panel over a tension rod and pull one bottom corner up and over the rod to expose the view during the day.

A creative approach to accessorizing is to take something intended for one use and repurpose it in a completely different way. For example, an

RIGHT:

It's always nice to set the table with care so guests feel special, even when entertaining in the kitchen.

OPPOSITE:

The legs of the unfinished farm table in the kitchen were stained, while the top was painted and then trimmed

with a wallpaper border. An unfinished hutch, which holds chinaware, was whitewashed with paint and stenciled with a blue check design to match the sofa fabric.

interesting wicker backpack holds fishing poles in corner of a room. Hooks, evenly placed along the hallway wall, solved the problem of no hall closet for coats. A variety of mismatched chinaware, tins, crockery, pitchers, small bottles, apothecary jars, and jelly glasses sitting on kitchen counters and windowsills make delightful containers for a spontaneous bouquet of wildflowers or weeds, like dandelions and buttercups.

Many things have the potential for a makeover and can look new and up-to-date by recovering and recycling. Replacing fabric and paint is the easiest way to unify a hodgepodge of mismatched items, elevating the most unsightly pieces from their humble beginnings. For example, the couple found a sofa at a Salvation Army store. They had never done a project like this but, taking it step by step, they figured it out and found how simple it was to cover the sofa with a blue-and-white-checked fabric using hot glue and a staple gun. "It was easier than we thought," they recall, "but we figured the sofa didn't cost much so we didn't have a lot to lose by trying." The coffee table was once a sleigh seat. They painted it to match the fabric and kitchen chairs. An old vinyl hassock was covered with the same fabric as the love seat, and a boat rope was tied around the middle in a nautical knot, with two shells hot-glued to each tied end of the rope. The chairs were all found in different yard sales and painted.

UPSCALE DOWNSIZING

DIY Projects

It's fun to experiment with decorative paint finishes like sponging, ragging, and spatter painting on chairs and other small accessories. Sometimes an old chair with peeling paint can look charming when left as is. Thompson's® House and Deck Stain with Water Seal® comes in many colors and provides an excellent finish for outdoor furniture, such as Adirondack chairs, allowing you to waterproof and add color all in one step.

Ordinary household items like sheets, pillowcases, and table covers are thrift-shop and yard-sale staples. They can be the beginning of a creative decorating scheme. Fabric dye brightens almost anything, and I love the variety of shades you can achieve with it. Believe it or not, tie-dyeing does not produce garish designs exclusively. I've used this technique to produce subtle pastels for a marbleized effect on plain white pillowcases. For mere pennies, you can tie-dye them in different shades of pale colors by not leaving the cloth too long in the dye bath. (Follow directions on the back of the fabric-dye box.) Add an unusual touch to the bedroom with a pile of pastel-dyed pillowcases.

OPPOSITE:
Tie-dyed pillowcases in soft pastel shades and an applique quilt lighten the heavy timber beams in the bedroom.

RIGHT:
Humble kitchen chairs were sponge-painted blue.

HOW TO SPONGE-PAINT

SPONGE-PAINTING IS THE EASIEST OF ALL THE FAUX-PAINTING TECHNIQUES AND IS GREAT FOR CREATING INTERESTING TEXTURE ON ANY PAINTED OBJECT.

1. Choose a water-based paint in a light color, preferably white. Coat the object with the paint and let dry.

2. Next, pour a small amount of a contrasting color into a small dish. (Cobalt blue is used in the photo below.)

3. Dip a natural sponge (found in a craft, paint, or hardware store) into the contrasting color. Starting at one edge of the object, begin pouncing the paint onto the white undercoat, leaving some white paint showing in a random pattern, until the object is covered. Keep going over the paint with feather-light pounces to blend and soften the texture.

4. Stand back and look over the item. If there are areas that need blending, continue until you are satisfied with the finished look. If you've applied too much of the dark color, wipe it away with a dry paper towel and, without adding more paint to your sponge, blend again with a pouncing motion.

5. Let dry completely. Coat the object with a clear water-based semi-gloss polyurethane to protect the paint and give the finished project a subtle sheen.

169

10

CREATIVE DESIGNS

TOWNHOUSE LIVING

A single man recently bought a simple townhouse on a busy street. He owns a successful flower and home-accessories shop in a resort town in New England. Tired of maintaining a large home, he downsized to avoid a lot of maintenance and chose this house because it's within walking distance of work. During the wedding season, this shop owner goes 24/7. "I have no outdoor space around the house and no time for entertaining, but I enjoy the outdoors on my walk to and from the shop," he explains. "I'm often asked where I got my sense of style. I had one of the greatest mentors: a well-respected decorator [and] the original owner of my shop. He was very kind to me and taught me a lot. His style was understated but elegant, and he was the master of decorating small spaces. If you paid attention, you got the best education by just being around him. And there have been others." He continues, "[A friend who was an] artist taught me about using the color white with fine English pine furniture. He was the first to create this look, and it's still a classic."

His advice to those who haven't a clue when it comes to decorating their new downsized home is this: "If you pay attention to what talented people are doing, you eventually gain the confidence to trust your instincts. By going with what I like and using the different ideas I've seen, I've developed my own sense of what is tasteful. Slowly, I acquired my own sense of style." When it comes to decorating your home, he suggests: "Go with what you like. Go with your gut feelings. What works in one room may not work in another." He laughs and notes, "There are no rules. What works for me is: bigger, and lots of it." He also thinks flowers can do so much for a home, no matter its size. You can always make your home look elegant with bouquets of all-white flowers. He recommends, "Use tons of lily of the valley. Buckets of it everywhere! And your home will have an intoxicating scent."

The house is sparsely furnished with the favorite things that survived the move. The homeowner admits, "This house probably should have been a teardown. But I love antique houses,

so I did a lot of work on it although only the kitchen and bathrooms were modernized. The rest was restored exactly as it was, as a cozy antique house."

He acknowledges, "I don't have time to decorate or fuss too much, because of my schedule." But each room seems effortlessly put together for comfort and visual interest. For example, he sticks to a mostly neutral palette, adding texture and a little pattern to the all-white basic color scheme. He says, "I live with color all day, and a neutral palette at home is a relief. It's restful." Accents of green from living plants add just enough refreshing color to suit him.

His furniture consists of classic pieces, like the overstuffed sofas in the living room. Some of his furniture was acquired years ago, like a set of upholstered leopard-skin dining chairs. He uses them in the small, captivatingly glamorous dining area created at one end of the kitchen. He explains,

UPSCALE DOWNSIZING

OPPOSITE:

A small upstairs bedroom under the eaves has its own bathroom. Simplicity is key to this homeowner's lifestyle. A clothes tree is practical when closet space is spare, and an inexpensive side table with a full-length cover provides hidden storage space.

BELOW:

The homeowner painted a checker-board pattern on the floor, applying it over original floorboards. The leopard-skin chairs are twenty-five years old and still look classic. Oversize mirrors, a wall of plates, and framed lithographs on the opposite wall delineate the dining area in the kitchen.

TIP: White walls and scrub-pine furniture are good choices if you're moving into a smaller space. They feel lighter, whereas a mahogany piece, in contrast, takes up more visual space.

"I don't have or need a separate dining room, but it's easy to take part of a room and make it look like a separate room by decorating as if it is a tiny room."

The walls and floors are painted glossy white throughout the house. The use of oversize, ornately framed mirrors adds opulence that contrasts with the intimacy of the small rooms. "I love the feeling of this house," he says. "In the winter, I gravitate to my cozy little living room. It's small and tucked in. I can spy what's cooking on the stove. I love it!"

This homeowner's choice of art is eclectic. "I like groupings of artwork with the same simple frames to tie them together," he says. He looks

at each area and creates vignettes with different objects to reflect his current interest, and changes things around at whim. For anyone who can't part with the things they've collected and love, this homeowner suggests allocating a small closet space to hold unused items. If you pare things down and keep them together in one self-contained place, you can't keep buying unless you're willing to get rid of something. Once you have the basic furniture, you can rearrange and change out the accessories from time to time to freshen things up. "Rooms shouldn't become stagnant," he recommends.

Aside from years of flower arranging, many travels to Palm Springs, California, have

enlightened this homeowner to the joys of color. He observes, "Strong, bright colors are everywhere. Orange is very important out there, and I've taken a few tips from California living to incorporate in the Northeast. For example, I've discovered that orange accent pieces can mix well with the traditional blue and white homes I'm more familiar with. Outdoor living, succulent gardens, [and] avocados all impact design there."

When it comes to entertaining in your new small home, this design expert suggests: "Entertain with what you have. . . . Use whatever is growing in your garden for a centerpiece. You should always make your home feel alive with cut flowers or

LEFT:

The all-white farmhouse-style kitchen is the largest and most used room in the house. It is simply accented with green growing plants, topiaries, and a pitcher of freshly cut lilies.

ABOVE:

A narrow sideboard is a versatile and interesting piece of furniture for holding table linens. Black-and-white lithographs fill the wall with matching sconces on each side. Clean accents of green and white are created with a bowl of Granny Smith apples, topiary, and succulents. It's inexpensive to create a display of interesting accessories such as these. The owner, a florist, always has a simple arrangement of fresh flowers on the table.

175

a living plant. A few stalks of fragrant lilies are especially welcoming in the entryway (if you have one) and living room. A small bouquet of roses on a bedside table is an easy and inexpensive way to feel pampered, and, when you have houseguests, there should be an arrangement in the guest room."

Whether he's styling a wedding or advising a homeowner on how to arrange a room, he says the key to success is the right mix: "A room will have character if you infuse it with something old and something new as well as something one of a kind. Style doesn't have to cost a bundle." And don't forget the fresh flowers!

BELOW:

An oversize mirror fills one wall of the living room, giving the illusion of space. The tobacco-colored walls warm the room.

OPPOSITE, ABOVE:

Moss and succulents in mercury glass–footed containers are used to create an interesting tablescape. Look for unusual chinaware, napkins, and place mats.

OPPOSITE, BELOW:

A wall-to-wall window seat is built into the upstairs landing, which is used as a home office. It's as long as two twin beds placed end to end and perfect for guests.

TIP: Take lots of photographs of nature, as well as architectural details, when you are traveling to another part of the country. It can be inspiring for your interior design when you return home. Go on house and garden tours in other areas when possible.

KEEPING YOUR SMALL HOME FRESH AND STYLISH

THIS DESIGN EXPERT OFFERS HIS TIPS FOR DECORATING ANY HOME, NO MATTER HOW SMALL.

1. The key to an interesting room is the right mix: old and new, like an antique piece with something modern. Try grouping similar things together as well. For example, when displayed together, clusters of neutral-colored art that are all framed similarly make a strong statement.

2. After you've downsized as much as possible for your comfort level, regularly edit your decorative accessories and pass some along to someone who might enjoy them, or donate the items to a worthy cause. It gives you a chance to freshen up any room and share beautiful things.

3. Use whatever you like for decorative accessories. Lots of books, for example, can be loosely "arranged," which makes it less intimidating for a guest to borrow one.

4. Start with a neutral background or a white room, and let the flowers and accessories bring in the color. Every room should also have some black in it. Black grounds a room.

5. For small rooms, oversize mirrors with heavy, ornate frames add opulence and visually enlarge the space.

6. Use what you have growing in your garden to make flower arrangements for your home. Lilies and roses are classic and last the longest. Lilies are nice in a foyer. A small tight bouquet of roses on a bedroom nightstand is a lovely touch. When putting bouquets together, try one or two types of flowers only, rather than a variety of flowers as an arrangement.

7. A house should smell good. Scented candles are lovely on an entryway table, and there should always be pretty soap in the bathrooms.

8. Assess your table linens before entertaining. It's inexpensive and, with so much to pick from, enormously satisfying to buy new place mats and napkins for a fresh new look or when you just want to try out a new color scheme.

9. Set a table with interesting props, like flower containers. Keep an arrangement low enough for guests to see over. Make creative groupings with candles.

AN URBAN APARTMENT

The owner of a 625-square-foot (58-square-meter) apartment wanted an innovative space that camouflaged any resemblance to an ordinary "white box" apartment devoid of architectural features. Trudy Dujardin and Price Connors, of Dujardin Design Associates, Inc. in Connecticut and Massachusetts, achieved that goal using materials and textures inspired both by the urban park nearby and the geometry of city buildings. Known for their inspired use of materials and their attention to detail, the design firm created a feeling of quiet elegance with a decidedly mid-century modern decor. By incorporating the owner's strong personal sense of style, the designers created an apartment that is at once stylish, sophisticated, and exceedingly comfortable.

Dujardin says, "While the footprint of the apartment is small, the owner wanted a dining area that feels like a separate room." To do this, they designed an intimate dining corner by delineating the space with curving walls and covering them with a rivet-design grasscloth. Dujardin continues, "A dropped ceiling makes a small space feel like a separate room, providing a bit of drama as well as a romantic feeling. Curved soffits allowed for the installation of recessed lighting, and a pendant chandelier casts interesting shadows." For the furniture, the designers chose a solid walnut table for its sinuous twist of movement that befits the space, subtly repeating the silhouette of the buildings seen outside the windows. The custom-made banquette and retro-inspired armchairs provide ample seating and complete the "room."

BELOW:

The living room of a 625-square-foot (58-square-meter) apartment is elegantly appointed with top-of-the-line materials and furnishings. Rough chiseled stone covers the main wall behind the sofa.

Using materials of different textures throughout the apartment creates another interesting feature. For example, in the living room, this design team used rough chiseled stone to cover the walls, a dramatic backdrop to the sleek-lined furniture. For the flooring, they chose sustainable bamboo in a dark zero-VOC finish. The exquisite, multi-textured area rug was designed in the 1970s by renowned textile designer Jack Lenor Larsen and adds just the right amount of color to complement the architectural details and quiet furnishings. Antique horse-blanket pillows punctuate the sofa. Dujardin and Connors are always mindful of the particular interests of their clients and incorporate it whenever possible, making each project unique to the owner's personality and lifestyle. For example, in this apartment, the owner's Far East travels inspired the wall hanging composed of eighteenth-century Tibetan Buddhist prayers written on bamboo.

OPPOSITE:

A curved wall and recessed lighting delineate an intimate dining corner.

LEFT, ABOVE:

A contemporary painting over a small desk picks up the persimmon color used as an accent throughout the apartment.

LEFT, BELOW:

Eighteenth-century Tibetan Buddhist prayers written on bamboo separate the dining corner from the living area. A wine cooler and storage are below.

The custom-made bedding is enhanced with decorative tape applied to mimic the Greek key motif found on a pair of bedside chests, which are adaptations of a James Mont design from the 1940s. Tripod lamps are reissues of a T. H. Robsjohn-Gibbings design from the 1950s. The recessed lighting casts a lovely glow on the persimmon silk wall covering from Phillip Jeffries. This material is especially exquisite with its delicate texture and rich color and infuses the room with a soft vibrancy.

A frosted sliding glass panel leads to a walk-in dressing area and, when opened, reveals a mirror built into the wall. The unique bronze parquet inlaid panel features a geometric composition in earth tones.

OPPOSITE:

A persimmon silk wall covering by Phillip Jeffries creates an elegant background on one bedroom wall. The Greek key motif on the side table is mimicked on the pillow and bedskirt trim.

REDESIGNING AN URBAN APARTMENT

MANY URBAN APARTMENTS LACK ARCHITECTURAL DETAILS AND PERSONALITY, BUT KEEP IN MIND THAT THE SPACE CAN BE RECONFIGURED. FOR LARGE PROJECTS, IT'S IMPORTANT TO HIRE A GOOD DESIGN TEAM THAT INCLUDES AN ARCHITECT.

1. Your goal is to forget that you're in a small space.

2. A plain, boxy apartment can turn into a classic, timeless, beautiful space by combining contemporary furniture and rare antiques with healthy building materials.

3. Sometimes walls can be removed to create an open, airy feeling. Half-walls can create visual dividers. When you can't change the footprint of an apartment, creating a curved wall (as Dujardin did) or a dropped ceiling can achieve your goals.

4. To make an apartment memorable and comfortable, use full-scale furniture and carefully chosen decorative objects. Create a major focal point in each room.

5. Architectural details, such as molding, columns, or wainscoting, can be added for visual interest.

6. A flexible seating arrangement is a good idea for accommodating big parties. A large table, for example, can provide a space for both work and dining. If you have only two comfortable chairs in the living room, pull dining chairs into the room to accommodate more people when needed.

7. Remember that good lighting and fixtures are as important as the furnishings.

LIVING WITH COLOR

Many people believe that painting the interior of a small house white expands the feeling of space. But this isn't always true. Some decorators ignore all the rules and reinvent a new look when it comes to their own homes, no matter the size. One such decorator loves to be surrounded by the items he's collected over the years during his worldwide travels and cannot imagine a home without lots of color. It works when the homeowner has a feel for how to marry all the things he loves with the vibrant colors that make him happy.

"For as long as I can remember, I've always been drawn to beautiful things," says interior designer Gary McBournie in the introduction to his book *Living Color: A Designer Works Magic with Traditional Interiors*, written by William Richards. "Gary is a happy guy," says Bill when describing McBournie, his partner in life and in business. Indeed, this couple seems to have found their sweet spot, and their home is a reflection of their attitude—filled with happy colors. Gary McBournie, Inc. is a residential interior design firm established in 1992. Based in Boston with offices in New York City and Palm Beach, Florida, they have projects all over the world. But the project they just finished for themselves could be their favorite.

Gary and Bill like beautiful things, and minimal living is definitely not for them. Perhaps you'll identify with their attitude when it came to decorating their country cottage. "We love to shop," says Bill, "so this may not be our last home, but when we design a house for ourselves, we have more freedom to try out new ideas, colors, etc. It adds a dimension to what we do for our clients." Gary observes, "We've been in this house for five years, but a house is never done. Traveling always gives us new ideas." Bill interjects, "We're like two kids in a candy store when we're shopping, especially in places like Marrakesh and the flea markets of Paris. We sold our past houses furnished, so moving into this

Custom-upholstered walls in the guest bedroom incorporate views of the garden with
its vintage floral fabric. The color scheme features soft oranges, blues, and greens
for a happy vibe.

cottage was easy. We could start from scratch with a whole new direction." Not many of us have this luxury. However, those who feel more comfortable surrounded by the things they've collected can learn from these professionals how to put a room together artfully.

Their H-shaped, ranch-style cottage is set in the middle of an acre of land. The landscaping, seen from every window, was an important project and the first one they tackled. They created a long shell-lined driveway as an approach to the house with well-trimmed hedges that flank a bright-blue door. That door opens onto a brick path that leads through a breathtaking garden that might easily be found in the countryside of England or the south of France, areas that influenced the planning of the garden. Like a separate room, it stops you in your tracks and allows you to decompress from wherever you've been. Like everything about the

BELOW:

An outdoor shower is a luxury, but if you have the space it's a great way to add a shower when you have only one bathroom. This bathroom is luxuriously outfitted with a reclaimed sink, a custom mirror, and a wooden anchor.

OPPOSITE:

This open-air porch was built to create the symmetrical H-shape of the house and expand the living space in warm weather. The furniture is a combination of vintage bamboo pieces, Parsons-style side tables with tops created from old plaques, an antique walnut table, and a mid-century server. The accessory pieces were primarily found in various antiques shops and auctions. Hanging light fixtures create a romantic ambience.

house, the garden looks as though it's always been here, lovingly taken care of over the years. A bench at the edge of the path enables them to sit amid the flowers and enjoy being in this space. For some people, their outdoor space is as important as the interior rooms. Keep this in mind when relocating.

Some places make you feel instantly at home, as if you'd always belonged there. Sometimes you walk into a house and some part of you responds in a way that awakens your senses. This one-story house is like that. It exudes cottage style, simply nestled into the landscape. Bill says, "We like the scale of the rooms. Houses with large rooms and an open floor plan aren't as appealing to us. We like the idea that rooms invite different activities that don't intrude on each other. If someone is reading in one room and someone else is watching television in another, each has privacy.

The dining room is between the kitchen and the outdoor living/dining room. A pair of cane-back armchairs and a set of apple-green chairs are decidedly mid-century modern. A framed Picasso lithograph hangs over the two-drawer cabinet (France, 1960). The brass eight-arm chandelier with white frosted-glass cylinder shades is Italian (circa 1960). The "Champagne on Pewterleaf" wall covering from Phillip Jeffries gives the room an elegant shimmer.

LEFT:
The blue door, set into a privacy hedge, leads from the shell driveway through the garden to the house. The door, an integral part of the design, suggests a "secret garden" beyond.

This is how early cottages were built." Gary adds, "My grandmother raised a large family in a modest turn-of-the-century-house in Boston, and she was my earliest design influence. She wasn't wealthy, but she brought a style and graciousness into her home. To this day, a down-filled cushion is a requisite of every room I design."

The house is less than 2,000 square feet (1,856 square meters), but it feels spacious because of the high ceiling in the living room, lots of light from many windows—all with garden views— and the exuberant color palette Gary is known for. His approach to color and patterns is one

with confidence, marrying the unexpected with surprisingly original results. "Orange is my favorite 'neutral,'" Gary notes. "I'm simply not a beige person, and as much as I've tried to create all-white, monochromatic rooms, they just don't work for me." Bill says their painted-white living room is a concession in this house, but it works with the colors and textures of the furniture, rugs, and artwork. Overall, there is a traditional approach to the furnishings that is at once comfortable, like a family home that has been reinterpreted with an eye for sophistication. It suits the owners' lifestyle right now. Vibrant blues, lime green, and, of course, orange

mix well with the mid-century modern furnishings and art. Some walls are covered with fabric. Others are given texture with faux finishes.

When they first saw it, the property was a mess, with paved macadam everywhere. Despite its rundown condition, the couple knew instantly that it was for them. The sprawling low building has the classic appeal of the 1930s and 1940s, instantly inviting and unpretentious. It sits, not regal or imposing, but situated into the landscape. Inside, the house unfolds little by little, an accumulation of rooms with nooks and hallways that you uncover as you go through it. The interior design is proof that these designers embrace the present as well as the past and that the best results are achieved when being open to both. If you are a traditionalist, you can learn much from the decorating tips that follow.

ABOVE:

The master bedroom reflects the exterior environment. The window drapery fabric from Marimekko extends across the wall behind the custom-designed bed from Gary McBournie. Walls are cross-glazed blue. Vintage Lucite and brass lamps complement walnut side tables.

OPPOSITE:

Gary loves to cook and designed the kitchen in scale with the rest of the house. The counter space around the room is walnut, but the island is marble. The orange-and-white-painted floor pattern is dramatically large and unexpected in a small kitchen.

DECORATING TIPS FROM A SEASONED PROFESSIONAL

GARY MCBOURNIE OFFERS HIS TIPS FOR DIY INTERIOR DESIGN.
(SEE PHOTOS OF HIS DESIGNS ON HIS WEBSITE: WWW.GMCBINC.COM.)

A WELL-THOUGHT-OUT FLOOR PLAN will be your road map to success. A measured drawing of the space will help you play with furniture size and placement. Graph paper and a measuring tape are essential.

FURNISHINGS ARE ONLY PART OF THE PUZZLE. Floor type and color, the texture of the walls and ceilings, and architectural details such as moldings, cornices, casings, and window trims, give a room gravitas.

A ROOM ISN'T COMFORTABLE if the furniture is wrong for the size of the room or height of the ceilings. Follow these simple rules: For high ceilings, use larger-scale upholstered furniture. For low ceilings, use longer, shorter upholstered furniture. Accentuate a room's height with tall, thin objects like floor lamps, bookcases, and open-arm chairs.

CREATE GROUPINGS. Consider the use of the room and make spaces that have different functions. In a living room, for example, avoid using just a sofa and two chairs as your only arrangement. Instead, consider placing a love seat or a pair of chairs at the other end of the room for another conversational area. In a bedroom, create a reading area with a chair and ottoman.

START WITH YOUR COLOR PALETTE. Gary uses nature for inspiration, but ideas can also come from art or fabric. Choose three to five colors, and don't be intimidated. Some of the colors may only show up in a pillow or a trim as accents.

THE COLORS OF ADJACENT ROOMS should relate to one another. Pull the paint color from one room to use in fabric for another. Keep trim the same color from room to room.

PAINT SAMPLE BOARDS and leave them out. See how they look together and in different lighting. Take time to properly sand, caulk, and prime walls and trim. There is a big payoff for the effort.

FILL YOUR UPHOLSTERY WITH DOWN or at least choose down-wrapped cushions. The luxury experience is well worth the cost. Use left over fabric from draperies, sofas, and chairs for throw pillows.

MOUNT CUSTOM IRON RODS and rings as high as possible. Decorate simple drapery panels with a contrast band, and use a double lining to minimize sun damage and darken a room. You can also install matchstick or bamboo blinds, or custom Roman shades, behind the draperies.

CREATE POOLS OF LIGHT WITH LAMPS. Avoid overhead lights. To create ambience, add dimmer switches to your electrical cords.

SMALL COCKTAIL OR SIDE TABLES and a set of nesting tables will allow guests to settle in and enjoy the space.

ACCESSORIES MAKE IT PERSONAL. Put shells, a pile of favorite books, old family photographs, a glass bowl, and anything reminiscent of childhood on display.

RIGHT:

After a trip to
Copenhagen, the
living room, with
its high ceiling, was
conceived with large
white space to reflect
the purity of that
country. The colors
of the furnishings
evoke a walk through
the spice market
of Marrakesh. The
captivating blue
glass mirror and
large brass Italian
Sputnik light fixture
came from the Palm
Beach Antique and
Design Center.

ACKNOWLEDGMENTS

I have been very lucky to make my living from creative challenges and to work with like-minded people all over the country. I would like to thank the following homeowners for telling their stories and lending their homes as examples of creative downsizing: Carol and Bob Miller; George Korn and Thomas Livingston; Michael Pelkey; Gary McBournie and Bill Richards; Ron and Debbie Lilly; Elizabeth English and Mark Donato; Mellie Cooper; and Michael Molinar. I would also like to thank the following interior designers whose work appears frequently in national magazines: Trudy Dujardin and Price Connors of Dujardin Design in Westport, CT, and Nantucket, MA; Christine Roughan of Roughan Interior Design in Weston, CT, and New York City; Kathleen Hay Designs in Nantucket, MA; and the architectural firm of Angus MacLeod Designs, which is located in Nantucket, Boston, and Ashville, NC. Also thanks to photographers Jeffrey Allen, Terry Pommett, Jane Beiles, and Jon Aron, as well as my wonderful agent, Linda Konner of Linda Konner Literary Agency.

I am especially grateful for two wonderful partners. The first is Terry Pommett, with whom I have produced several books and dozens of magazine articles. He is a dream to work with. The second is my husband, Jon Aron, who is my "go-to person" in all things professional and personal and who I count on to keep me sane.

ABOUT THE AUTHOR

Leslie Linsley is one of the best-known authors of crafts, decorating, and home-style books, which number over sixty titles, including *Country Living Aged to Perfection* and *Country Living Salvage Style*. Her articles have appeared on HGTV online and in numerous magazines, including *Family Circle* (where she was a contributing craft editor from 1990-2005), *Woman's Day*, *Country Living*, *Redbook*, *New York*, *House Beautiful*, *Elle Decor*, *Good Housekeeping*, *Martha Stewart Living*, and *O*. Guest appearances include *Oprah*, *Today*, *Good Morning America*, HSN, QVC, and HGTV. Leslie's branded products are sold through her own department at the Marine Home Center in Nantucket. Leslie has also served as a media spokesperson for the following companies, among others: Lowe's, 3M, Sherwin-Williams, Waverly, and Hunter Douglas. Learn more about her at leslielinsley.com and leslielinsley.com/blog. She lives on Nantucket Island, MA.

PHOTO CREDITS

INDEX

Note: Page numbers in *italics* indicate captions.